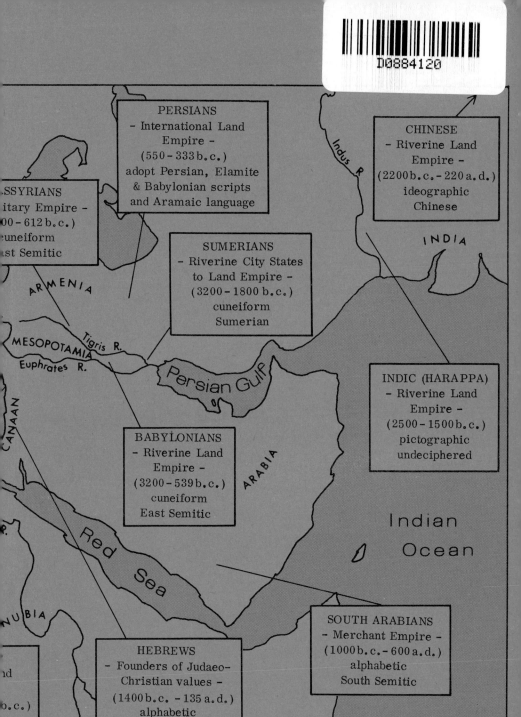

PERSIANS
- International Land
Empire -
(550 - 333 b.c.)
adopt Persian, Elamite
& Babylonian scripts
and Aramaic language

CHINESE
- Riverine Land
Empire -
(2200 b.c. - 220 a.d.)
ideographic
Chinese

SSYRIANS
itary Empire -
00 - 612 b.c.)
uneiform
st Semitic

INDIA

SUMERIANS
- Riverine City States
to Land Empire -
(3200 - 1800 b.c.)
cuneiform
Sumerian

ARMENIA

Tigris R.

MESOPOTAMIA

Euphrates R.

Persian Gulf

INDIC (HARAPPA)
- Riverine Land
Empire -
(2500 - 1500 b.c.)
pictographic
undeciphered

CANAAN

BABYLONIANS
- Riverine Land
Empire -
(3200 - 539 b.c.)
cuneiform
East Semitic

ARABIA

Indian
Ocean

Red Sea

Indus R.

NUBIA

HEBREWS
- Founders of Judaeo-
Christian values -
(1400 b.c. - 135 a.d.)
alphabetic
Northwest Semitic

SOUTH ARABIANS
- Merchant Empire -
(1000 b.c. - 600 a.d.)
alphabetic
South Semitic

R.

nd

b.c.)

tic

BEFORE COLUMBUS
Links Between the Old World
and Ancient America

BEFORE COLUMBUS

LINKS BETWEEN THE

OLD WORLD AND ANCIENT AMERICA

by CYRUS H. GORDON

Crown Publishers, Inc. New York

The maps on pages 71, 72, 74, 75 are from *Maps of the Ancient Sea Kings:
Evidence of Advanced Civilization in the Ice Age* by Charles H. Hapgood.
Copyright © 1966 by the author. Reproduced by permission of
Chilton Book Company, Philadelphia.

*All translations from the Old World languages have been controlled by the author
from the original sources.*

Dedicated to

JULES PICCUS

whose insight and initiative
touched off the chain reaction

CONTENTS

LIST OF ILLUSTRATIONS

ACKNOWLEDGMENTS

F O R T H E moral and material support that has made this book possible I am indebted to Mrs. Noma Copley, Mrs. Betty Ellis, Mr. Carl Landegger, Jr., Mrs. Helen Slosberg and especially to Mr. and Mrs. Eugene Grant.

My able research assistant, Mrs. Edith Creter, helped in innumerable details, and prepared the final typescript for press.

I am also grateful to Mr. John Lawrenz, a graduate fellow in Mediterranean Studies at Brandeis University, for drawing the charts that should help the reader visualize an assortment of geographic, chronologic, ethnographic and cultural data. Miss Deborah J. Gordon helped me assemble the illustrations, and Mr. Nicholas J. Cafarelli III facilitated my task by tracking down some elusive references.

Anyone aware of the irrational hostilities evoked by the topic of this book knows that it could be written only in an intelligent and sympathetic atmosphere. My wife Joan provided that atmosphere.

In Chapter VI the reader will learn why this book is dedicated to Professor Jules Piccus. My candle is shedding light because he ignited it.

C.H.G.

BEFORE COLUMBUS

Links Between the Old World

and Ancient America

INTRODUCTION

T H I S B O O K is the result of an inquiry into the origin and character of world civilization in which we are now playing a prominent role. Our conclusions should therefore help us more fully to understand ourselves, our place in the order of things and our responsibilities.

The chapters that follow show how various avenues of approach point to the same conclusion: that for thousands of years men have been in contact with other men at the ends of the earth, influencing each other's ways of life, and producing thereby an intertwined network of developed regional cultures. We shall be as specific as possible about what was transmitted—and when, where, how, why and by whom the transmission was effected. Depending on the nature and extent of the evidence, our conclusions along the way will be more general or more specific. But we shall stick to the facts and their direct implications, without erecting a hypothetical structure. What emerges should reflect the exercise of perception, not flights of fancy.

Civilized nations may differ as to location, race, language, historic origins and creativity—but they are all connected through mixture, contact, both outright and modified borrowing, and stimulus diffusion. The latter is particularly important though easily missed. It refers to the spread of ideas, which are implemented along independent lines by the borrower. If we hear that another nation has scored a breakthrough in space travel by means of a secretly designed vehicle, we are impelled to construct such a vehicle even though our engineers have to design it and work out the details from scratch. As a result, the new spacecraft may look entirely different from the one that inspired it through stimulus diffusion. If a thousand years from now, archeologists should unearth the two spacecrafts and because of their numerous differences should attribute both of them to independent invention, they would be essentially wrong even though to the superficial observer they might appear right. For the idea is the essence; the execution is secondary.

Primitive societies may be independent of each other. The boomerang-throwing aborigines of Australia had a culture independent of, and quite different from, the igloo-building Eskimos. But all high, technologically developed civilizations are the result of international stimulation so that all of them are connected by what they have learned from each other. China heard about casting bronze from the West; and what impelled China to invent her own system of writing was the diffusion of the idea of writing from the Near East. As we shall see, not even the highly developed civilizations of pre-Columbian Mesoamerica were outside the network of intertwined world cultures. Isolation may produce stable, but not innovative, societies. This is true just as much today as it was in antiquity. Nobel prizes are awarded to creative spirits whose achievements have been made possible by international stimulation; they are not won by the inhabitants of remote deserts, oases and mountaintops.

Our method is straightforward. We shall follow the primary sources to their simple and direct logical conclusions, unhampered by opinion that runs counter to the primary sources. For this reason we will not be concerned with any Gallup Poll type of approach; 49 percent support does not make anything necessarily wrong; nor does 51 percent support make it necessarily right. (The same holds for more extreme percentages, like 10 and 90 percent instead of 49 and 51 percent.) Nor are we committed to any school of thought such as "diffusionism" on the one hand or "independent inventionism" on the other. Whether we attribute any particular phenomenon to diffusion or to independent invention will depend on the evidence in the specific instance. Parallel occurrences of a simple element may be due to independent invention. The existence of houses in the New and Old Worlds is by itself no evi-

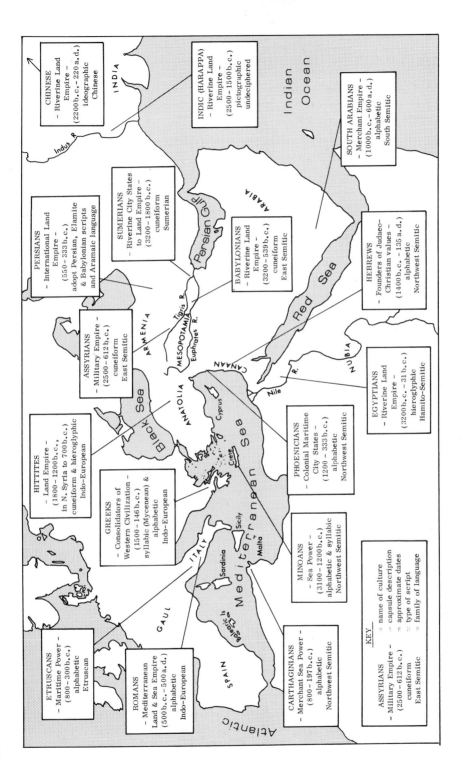

OLD WORLD CIVILIZATIONS

CHINESE
– Riverine Land Empire –
(2200 b.c. – 220 a.d.)
ideographic
Chinese

INDIC (HARAPPA)
– Riverine Land Empire –
(2500 – 1500 b.c.)
pictographic
undeciphered

SOUTH ARABIANS
– Merchant Empire –
(1000 b.c. – 600 a.d.)
alphabetic
South Semitic

PERSIANS
– International Land Empire –
(550 – 333 b.c.)
adopt Persian, Elamite
& Babylonian scripts
and Aramaic language

SUMERIANS
– Riverine City States to Land Empire –
(3200 – 1800 b.c.)
cuneiform
Sumerian

BABYLONIANS
– Riverine Land Empire –
(3200 – 539 b.c.)
cuneiform
East Semitic

HEBREWS
– Founders of Judaeo-Christian values –
(1400 b.c. – 135 a.d.)
alphabetic
Northwest Semitic

ASSYRIANS
– Military Empire –
(2500 – 612 b.c.)
cuneiform
East Semitic

EGYPTIANS
– Riverine Land Empire –
(3200 b.c. – 31 b.c.)
hieroglyphic
Hamito-Semitic

HITTITES
– Land Empire –
(1800 – 1200 b.c.,
in N. Syria to 700 b.c.)
cuneiform & hieroglyphic
Indo-European

PHOENICIANS
– Colonial Maritime City States –
(1200 – 333 b.c.)
alphabetic
Northwest Semitic

GREEKS
– Consolidators of Western Civilization –
(1500 – 146 b.c.)
syllabic (Mycenean) & alphabetic
Indo-European

MINOANS
– Sea Power –
(3100 – 1200 b.c.)
alphabetic & syllabic
Northwest Semitic

ETRUSCANS
– Maritime Power –
(800 – 300 b.c.)
alphabetic
Etruscan

ROMANS
– Mediterranean Land & Sea Empire –
(500 b.c. – 500 a.d.)
alphabetic
Indo-European

CARTHAGINIANS
– Merchant Sea Power –
(800 – 197 b.c.)
alphabetic
Northwest Semitic

KEY

ASSYRIANS – = name of culture
– Military Empire – = capsule description
(2500 – 612 b.c.) = approximate dates
cuneiform = type of script
East Semitic = family of language

Geographic labels: INDIA, Indus R., Indian Ocean, ARABIA, Persian Gulf, Red Sea, ARMENIA, Tigris R., MESOPOTAMIA, Euphrates R., ANATOLIA, Cyprus, CANAAN, Nile R., NUBIA, Black Sea, Crete, Mediterranean Sea, ITALY, Sicily, Malta, Sardinia, GAUL, Balearic Is., SPAIN, Atlantic

dence for contact, because men everywhere tend to provide shelter for themselves. However, Old and New World clusters of monumental stone pyramids and hypostyle [1] temples adorned with sculptured texts and reliefs plus painting (and scores of other shared details) infer a substantial degree of diffusion in direct proportion to the number of shared elements. The presence of stone knives in two communities by itself may have resulted from independent invention. But the presence of a highly complex mechanism such as color TV in two communities at opposite ends of the earth is due to diffusion.

Cultural indebtedness need in no way detract from the creativity of the borrower. Nothing comes out of nothing. People who have learned little have produced little of outstanding merit. Creative people are those who build constructively on the foundation of what they have acquired from others. Our background is a matter of time, place and luck; our achievement is what we do with it. This is as true of nations as it is of individuals.

We shall stress the positive, for negative evidence is of little value. For example, the Chinese rejected the milking of animals and the whole gamut of dairy activities. This does not mean that they lived in a world isolated from men who drank milk and ate butter, cheese and other dairy products. Our culture is shaped by what we reject as well as by what we accept, and sometimes what we reject is the more important. The Hebrew acceptance of Phoenician architecture turned out to be less significant than their rejection of Phoenician religion including human sacrifice. But the absence of human sacrifice in Israel does not imply any lack of contact with Phoenicia. We need not belabor the point that the absence of pyramids in Palestine does not disprove contact between Egypt and ancient Israel. By the same token the virtual [2] lack of wheels in pre-Columbian America does not, for reasons that we shall point out later, disprove contacts between the Old World and ancient America.

Since the transmission of culture must take place in time (as well as in place and through specific people), chronology is important. Precisely datable inscriptions are the best kind of evidence; but there are other means at our disposal for obtaining relative or approximate dates. Stratigraphy provides chronological sequences: what is found in a lower stratum precedes what is found in the stratum above it. Stylistically, artifacts of a given category can often be arranged in a more or less chronological order. But stratigraphy and style provide relative (not absolute) chronology. Absolute chronology will be provided with a diminishing margin of error by new techniques such as Carbon-14 (for organic materials) and thermoluminescence (for ceramics). Dendrochronology (based on tree rings), varves (laminations of soil deposited yearly by seasonal waters) and many other methods have been used, and could be employed with increasing exactitude as the years go by. But in the problem before us we must recognize to what extent borrowed elements need be related chronologically to their prototypes. The Washington Monument and Bunker Hill Monument are inspired by the obelisks of Egypt. That these American borrowings were constructed thousands of years after the Egyptian originals were built poses no problem because we know that the ancient obelisks are still in existence and have been imitated here in modern times. To say that the step pyramids of the Near East are unconnected with the Mesoamerican step pyramids simply because the latter were built thousands of years after the Egyptian Step Pyramid at Saqqara and after the heyday of the step pyramids, known as ziggurats in Mesopotamia, is irrelevant because the ziggurats and pyramids were still used by the pagans in the Near East during the early Christian centuries when the American pyramids were built. Moreover, the pyramids of Egypt, like the obelisks, are still imitated in the New World—even as the Madeleine in Paris and countless old bank buildings in the U.S.A. were in modern times patterned after classical Greek architecture in general, and the Parthenon in particular.

The preponderance of Old World material in this book is derived from the Near East and Mediterranean because my professional competence lies primarily in those areas. An Indologist undertaking this task would have stressed India, just as a Sinologist would have drawn more data from China.[3] Emphasis on any one area has its dangers unless we understand the global nature of the problem. The Near East (and Mediterranean) is one of the most important seminal areas in the history of world civilization—perhaps it is *the* most important one —but it is not the only one, as we shall repeatedly have occasion to note. Because we happen to know more about one area than another does not mean that we have to be one-sided in our judgment.

Ours is a subject that will continue to raise hackles for some time to come. Unpleasant though this may be, it is the measure of its importance. Many still maintain that man in the Western Hemisphere, prior to Columbus, developed civilizations quite independently of the Old World. Of late, a number of New World archeologists have for cogent reasons come to admit ancient Pacific crossings, but refuse to countenance Atlantic crossings. If you read this book carefully and completely, you will not only find proof of transatlantic communication in antiquity, but you will also see how the existence of an ancient global ecumene affects our understanding of the development and character of Western civilization in the Old World. We are in the course of learning about ourselves, as well as about the Indian cultures of America before Columbus.

Cyrus H. Gordon
Brookline, Mass.
15 September 1970

Chapter I

MESOAMERICANS
PORTRAYED BY THEIR
OWN SCULPTORS

CIVILIZATIONS OFTEN specialize in products which they turn out in prodigious quantities. Our American culture manufactures cars in far greater numbers than other cultures have produced their vehicles. No civilization ever turned out wagons or even wheelbarrows in anything like the number of automobiles coming off the assembly lines in Detroit. Near Eastern civilizations have since Neolithic times left masses of pottery that defy reckoning. Mesopotamia produced seal cylinders and clay tablets by the myriads. Ancient Mesoamerica fortunately produced hundreds of thousands of sculptures often showing human types quite vividly. Most of the sculptured portraits are of clay: a plastic medium that enabled the artists to achieve, with minimum difficulty, maximum expressiveness.

One would expect that the people portrayed were "Indians." But what is an "Indian"? The only definition that makes sense is "an American Indian is any member of the various groups of people inhabiting North and South America when Columbus reached the Western Hemisphere A.D. 1492." In Middle America there are many full-blooded Indian communities in various regions, such as the Aztec and Maya areas. The remarkable fact of the countless Mesoamerican ceramic figurines is that they portray few, if any, American Indian types (such as the Aztec or Maya) before A.D. 300. Those that appear prior to that date (and many that appear for a thousand years thereafter) belong to other races such as Far Eastern, African Negro and Caucasian.

Among the latter are a number of Mediterranean types, especially Semites.

The evidence for the preceding is on record in an important and handsomely illustrated book by Alexander von Wuthenau, *The Art of Terracotta Pottery in Pre-Columbian Central and South America* (Crown Publishers, Inc., New York, 1970). We shall review some of the ceramic sculptures to get an idea of their implications.

We start with the large Mixtec Negro head from Oaxaca. It is post-classical,[3a] 18 centimeters high and belongs to the Josue Saenz Collection in Mexico. The black color and the features, such as the thick lips, leave no doubt in anyone's mind that the artist has portrayed a Negro. No artist can "invent" authentic races of mankind, such as the types we are examining. The implication is simply that early America was the meeting ground of various races of men from the Old World who were eventually absorbed into the modern Indian populations.

The group of varied sculptured heads is of interest in different ways. The upper heads (*a* [13 centimeters high] and *b* [about 17 centimeters high]) are early classical stylized negroid types from Veracruz, with scar-tattooing, which is practiced widely in Africa. When people migrate, they transport cultural traits from their old home to the new. Accordingly the presence of African Negroes in early America implies some sort of cultural impact, hardly confined to tattooing. On the lower left (*c* [about 19 centimeters high]) is a late classical dancer wearing an ornate headdress; here we are dealing with a type that is readily recognized as Indian. Earlier in date is the old man to the right (*d* [about 15 centimeters high, in the Tulane University Collection]): a Near Easterner, who might be Semitic but looks more like an aged Armenian. This plate illustrates the nature of the problem: in early classical times, the Mesoamerican scene was complex, with Caucasians from Eurasia and blacks from Africa, but also with the prevailing Indian types represented by the ancient artists.

It is important for us to be familiar with the true Indian types (that *first* appear in any significant number around A.D. 300) if we are to speak of the non-Indian physiognomies that appear in ancient America. On this plate, *a* and *c* (about 17 centimeters high) are two of the handsomest classical representations of Indians (from Veracruz) such as those that can be seen today in Mexico. The girl (*a*) and the man

Postclassical Mixtec Negro Head from Oaxaca, Mexico.

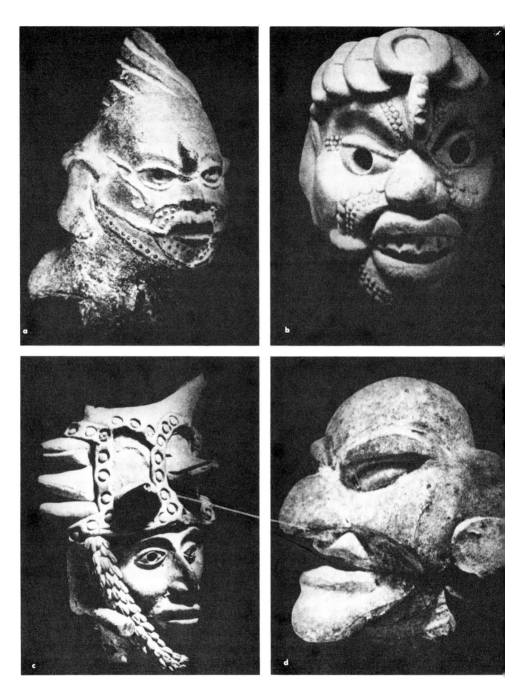

(a), (b) Highly stylized negroid heads with scar tattooing from Veracruz, Early Classical; (c) Late Classical Head of Dancer with ornate headdress; (d) Early East Mediterranean type (Armenian?).

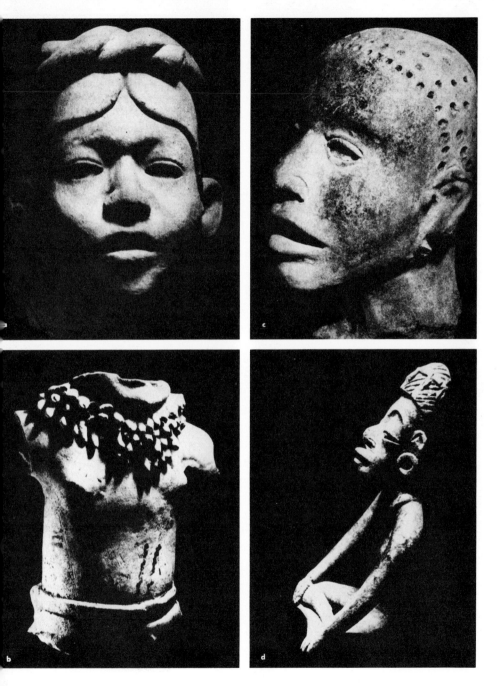

(a), (c) Classical Veracruz Indian types; (b) Classical Totonac dancer's torso; (d) seated negroid figure of Classical Period.

(*c*), in spite of some stylization—for instance, in the treatment of the eyes—are remarkably lifelike and expressive, and they rank among the finest pre-Columbian portraits. The nude torso of a classical Totonac girl adorned with a fancy necklace is portrayed on the lower left (*b* [21 centimeters high, in the Von Wuthenau Collection]). To the right (*d* [about 17 centimeters high, in the Stavenhagen Collection]) is a sitting woman (classical period) whose features appear more typical of black Africa than of Indian America.

From the Maya area of Iximché, in the province of Chimaltenango (Guatemala), comes a superb incense burner, probably of preclassical date. It is 33.5 centimeters high and belongs to the Musée de l'Homme in Paris. Everything about the sculptured head—nose, beard, expression—would fit a Northwest Semite. Whether he was a Phoenician, Syrian, Israelite, Greek or even an Etruscan is not important, for delving into such problems often degenerates into unprofitable hyperfinesse. If we be impelled to define him specifically, we may tentatively call him "an ancient Mediterranean merchant prince." From the Early Iron Age into Roman times, people of his type maintained creative contacts with middle America. He typifies an important group of the merchant mariners who linked the Mediterranean with the New World. His motives may have been trade, but trade for him meant the development as well as exchange of natural resources—all of which required the spread of science and technology. No physical anthropologist will try to change his classification from Mediterranean to American Indian. And the incense burner is related to similar ones from Veracruz. Accordingly in our "merchant prince" we have a specific link between preclassical Mesoamerica and the ancient Mediterranean.

In the private collection of Alexander von Wuthenau is a Mayan head, larger than life-size, portraying a pensive, bearded Semite. The dolichocephalic ("long-headed") type fits the Near East well. He resembles certain European Jews, but he is more like many Yemenite Jews. In Maya fashion his nose appears to extend up to the middle of his forehead.[4] This Maya custom is best explained as an exaggerated imitation of the prominent nose that characterizes so many Near Eastern types. It was precisely because men like the Mediterranean merchant princes were aristocrats in the Mesoamerican Order that their features were emulated by their Maya Indian successors.

Mediterranean Merchant Prince (ca. A.D. *300) from Iximché, Chimaltenango, Guatemala.*

Mayan head (greater than life-size) in the Von Wuthenau Collection.

During the transitional periods between antiquity and A.D. 1492, miscegenation brought about race mixture in which the Indian factors predominated. Some of the prevailing "American Indian" types swept southward from what is now the U.S.A. as conquerors. They were less civilized than many of their Mesoamerican victims, whose civilization they absorbed and developed.

The old view among Americanists had it that North and South America was peopled exclusively by savages that came across the Bering Straits in waves, starting in the Stone Age about 30,000 years ago. That early migrations took place across the Straits is not being questioned. The untenable aspect of the old view is that it disallows the other routes whereby people came to these shores before Columbus, or before the Vikings, around A.D. 1000. Primitive hunters are supposed to have moved south through Alaska, Canada and the United States and, without any outside stimulus, they are credited with the independent invention of numerous technologies long familiar in the Old World. A standard approach has it that all high civilizations except those in America were (or at least might be) connected through diffusion:

"All the European and Asian centers of civilization, from Rome to Japan, developed in direct or indirect contact with each other. Ideas, inventions, knowledge and goods circulated among them for thousands of years, enriching the heritage of all. Only Mexico and Peru remained outside the cultural pool." [5] But America was held to stand completely apart: "The most remarkable thing about the ancient American civilizations, however, was their independent development. Hidden behind their oceans, they had grown from the simplest beginnings with little help from each other and probably none of importance from the Old World." [6]

And yet there was evidence that the total isolation of America could not be so. Ancient Japanese pottery found in Ecuador forced a reappraisal at least to the extent of transpacific crossings.[7] Moreover, physical anthropology shows that: ". . . American Indian groups show a great deal of variation. In general the farther they live from the Bering Strait—and thus the earlier they can be presumed to have left Asia—the less Mongoloid they look, some of them possessing strikingly prominent noses, long heads or wavy hair, in contrast to the flat noses, round heads and straight hair that the typical Mongolians have today." [8]

An early group of faces is aptly described by Von Wuthenau as "a collection of Semitic types." From left to right they come from Guerrero, Veracruz, Tlatilco, the Maya area (the object is an incense burner), Nayarit, and Chiapas (a mask). All except the Nayarit figure are preclassical. (The Guerrero head is 13.5 centimeters high; the one from Chiapas is 14 centimeters high.) The beards and prominent noses point to Semitic rather than Indian subjects.

There is an interesting group of nine small heads from Guerrero (*a:* 5 centimeters; *b:* 5.6; *c:* 6.5; *d:* 5.2; *e:* 5.6; *f:* 6; *g:* 5.6; *h:* 5; *i:* 7). Most of them are preclassical, and the absence of Indian types among them is striking. They are remarkably varied and among them is one (*b*) that Von Wuthenau identifies with the Ainu—the hairy white aborigines of Japan. The Ainu are now a dwindling minority, but they were more numerous and widespread in antiquity and may well have had a role in the migrations and diffusion of culture across the Pacific.

The testimony of ancient American sculpture is complex but clear to this extent: Long before the Vikings reached America around A.D. 1000, Mesoamerica had long been the scene of the intermingling of different populations from across the Atlantic and Pacific oceans. Some of the most creative people in America came from the Near East; but no one group monopolized the scene. Caucasians from one end of Eurasia to the other came; Negroes, from Africa; Mongolians of Chinese and Japanese types, from the Far East; from the Mediterranean at different times came various Semites including Phoenicians and Carthaginians, as well as Egyptians, Greeks, Etruscans, Romans and still others. In general the main consequence was the mingling of highly civilized people from all over the world, creating on American soil, through the pooling of their cultural resources, a galaxy of brilliant Mesoamerican civilizations, whose final phases are known to us as Inca, Maya and Aztec. In culture, as in the physical universe, out of nothing comes nothing. The breathtaking achievements of the Mesoamericans could not be, and were not, the works of savages who lifted themselves up by their bootstraps. Instead they are the culminations of mingled strands of civilization brought to these shores by a variety of talented people from Europe, Africa and Asia.

There is no basis for saying that the people of preclassical Mesoamerica are a total mystery, or that they are simply the descendants of

Statuette from the Museo de Prehistoria, Valencia, featuring the nose reaching high on the forehead.

Early portrayals from (LEFT TO RIGHT) *Guerrero, Veracruz, Tlatilco, Maya (incense burner), Nayarit (fragment) and Chiapas (mask). All are Preclassical except the Nayarit figurine. None of the types are those of known Indian groups. Von Wuthenau stresses their Semitic features.*

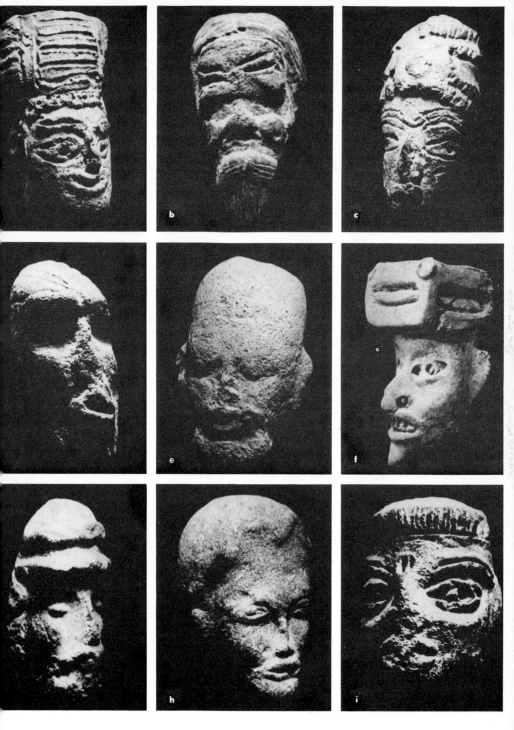

Guerrero heads, mainly Preclassical; all un-Indian. Of special interest is b, which has been compared with the hairy Caucasian Ainu of Japan.

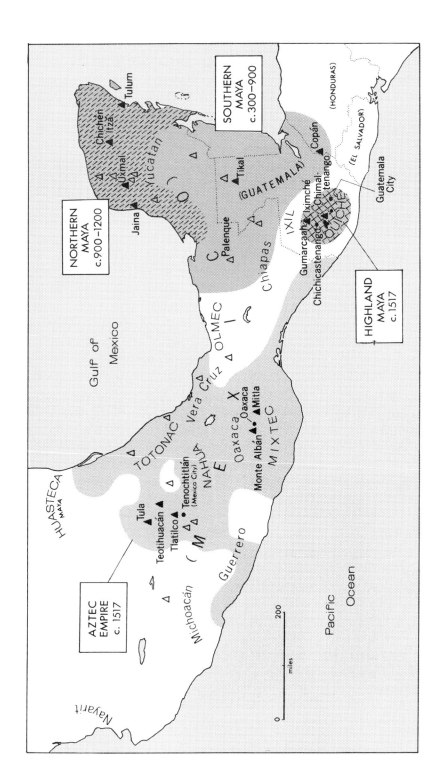

MESOAMERICA

AZTEC
EMPIRE
c. 1517

NORTHERN
MAYA
c. 900–1200

SOUTHERN
MAYA
c. 300–900

HIGHLAND
MAYA
c. 1517

Tulum

Chichén
Itzá

Uxmal

Yucatán

Jaina

Palenque

Chiapas

Tikal

(GUATEMALA)

IXIL

QUICHÉ

Copán

Chimal-
tenango

Iximché

Chichicastenango

Gumarcaah

Guatemala
City

(HONDURAS)

(EL SALVADOR)

Gulf of
Mexico

OLMEC

Vera Cruz

TOTONAC

HUASTECA
MAYA

Tula

Teotihuacán

Tlatilco

Tenochtitlán
(Mexico City)

NAHUA

M

Michoacán

Guerrero

Oaxaca
Monte Albán

Oaxaca
Mitla

MIXTEC

Nayarit

Pacific
Ocean

0   200
miles

Paleolithic hunters who wandered south from the Bering Straits, or that none of them came to Middle America across the Pacific and Atlantic. We know who they were racially from countless portrayals by ancient American sculptors. They definitely came across both oceans in pre-Columbian times. In fact, prior to A.D. 300, there is hardly any trace of types that we can call "Indian" among the ceramic portraits assembled by Von Wuthenau.

We need not base our conclusions on the sculptured portraits alone. There are other independent lines of evidence, and they all point in the same direction.[9]

We shall now turn to historic texts of classical Old World antiquity, which will help us pave the way for reconstructing the unified history of both the Eastern and Western Hemispheres.

Prehistoric and primitive men may have "invented" in isolation a number of ways of life belonging to the domain of cultural anthropology. For historians of civilized man, however, the entire globe has for thousands of years constituted One World. If high independently invented civilizations have existed, they were not on this planet.

Chapter II

THE TESTIMONY
OF GREEK AUTHORS

M A N K I N D   I S   R E B E L L I O U S by nature. This is one of the insights of the early chapters of Genesis narrating how our first ancestors defied God and ate of the forbidden fruit. Such myths contain more profound truth than many a tome of *vera historia.*

We are still rebellious but, unlike Adam and Eve, not always creatively so. In disobeying, they are represented as opening the minds of the human race to knowledge, raising us above the animals by bequeathing to us, their descendants, the thirst and capacity for knowledge—hitherto a divine prerogative. But the human race has since then often rebelled destructively. By turning our backs on our cultural heritage, we throw away our knowledge of the past and the precious spoils of time, and lose our bearings. A meaningful course must have not only a goal ahead, and our present location, but also the point of departure and the direction of the voyage that has brought us where we are.

Today it is all too common for the descendants of the most civilized men to lose the great cultures of their ancestors. Communist China is rapidly losing its role as a repository of the great Confucian tradition. In India, the bright young men go into fields like engineering, so that the old pundits are impoverished for lack of students to support them, and the great Sanskrit tradition is slipping fast. The modern university-trained Arab youth is no longer attracted to the Qoran (Koran) and the Arab classics, so that we often run into the phenomenon of Arab intellectuals who are not at home in the Arabic literature in which

Arab greatness is enshrined. The Turkish revolution under Mustafa Kemal in the 1920s abolished the traditional Arab script and substituted the Latin alphabet, so that the language continues, but none except the old can read Turkish books printed before 1928.

This has happened before in history many times. At the height of their glory, the Persians left royal inscriptions in their own Persian language and in their own Persian cuneiform script. The continuity of the people and of the language was not enough to preserve any knowledge of the ancient script. Modern Western scholars had to decipher the Old Persian inscriptions by the help of clues from other forms of the Persian language, and from the factual data preserved in Greek classics.

The same thing took place in Egypt. The people live on, and at least the native Coptic Church of Egypt preserves the ancient Egyptian language—but in a different script: a modification of the Greek alphabet. So the same situation developed in Egypt as in Persia: nobody could read the ancient inscriptions in which the glories of a brilliant past were recorded. By clues from Coptic and from Greek and Latin literature, modern savants of the West deciphered hieroglyphic Egyptian.[10]

Lest we sit in the seat of the scornful, let us reflect on the remissness of our own communities where the typical university graduate is hardly knowledgeable in the classics, which lie at the roots of his own culture. We do not refer only to the Latin, Greek and Hebrew languages, but even to the contents of their literatures which are available in translation.

How abysmal our ignorance is, is described by the term "collective amnesia": when mankind as a whole forgets the experience of the race. This book would never have had to be written were it not that mankind as a whole has forgotten major chapters of its history. If there were no evidence for restoring it, the subject would belong in the realm of speculation instead of historic reconstruction. But we have the same kind of evidence for regaining the history of ancient America as we had in the cases of Persia, Egypt and other forgotten civilizations: the testimony of the Hebrew, Greek and Latin classics, to which we may add the monuments and deciphered literatures of the Egyptians, Sumerians, Assyro-Babylonians, Hittites, Persians, Ugaritans, Minoans, Mycenaeans and so forth.

If we have forgotten what our classics tell us about ancient America, it is not the old sources that are at fault, but our own wilful blindness that has brought us into collective amnesia. Fortunately, however, ignorance is a curable disease.

The Greek sources happen to be the best, though not the oldest at our disposal. We shall start with the straightforward historical references before considering other kinds of literary sources that may contain kernels of historic truth but are overlaid with myth and legend. Not everything written as history is true. For this reason it is necessary to weigh sources against each other to determine what the balance of the evidence is. In examining the following evidence, we shall keep in mind that the Greek authors were not simply copying each other, but to the contrary there is a series of texts that points to an awareness of transatlantic contacts in antiquity based on various incidents, developments and traditions in different periods.

In the fourth century B.C. a Greek writer named Theopompus mentions an enormous "continent," outside the Old World, inhabited by exotic people living according to the strangest life-styles.[11] He cannot mean the Azores, Canaries, Madeira or Cape Verde Islands, for he regards the Old World continents as mere "islands." (Old Mediterranean people used the term "island" to mean any land mass that can be reached by sea—even huge continents—as is natural for mariners who, on reaching some shore, cannot tell whether they have come to a large island or a whole continent. Columbus himself felt sure that Cuba was the mainland!) The very strange people inhabiting the immense "island" would certainly fit America better than the British Isles or what we know of the Cassiterides ("The Tin Islands") which was populated by "enterprising people who occupy themselves with commerce" as a Latin author, Avienus, describes them.[12]

A collection of ancient Greek "Believe-It-or-Not" reports is called *Concerning Marvelous Things Heard* and attributed to Aristotle who lived in the fourth century B.C. Modern scholars are often inclined to attribute it to Aristotle's school rather than to the master himself. Section 84 of the collection deals with an "island" with navigable rivers discovered by the Carthaginians. Carthaginians went there, some to stay. To prevent an exodus that might shift prosperity from Carthage to that "island" the chief of the Carthaginians announced the death penalty for any planning to sail there. Moreover, all the inhabitants were killed so as to keep the information secret.[13]

The element of navigable rivers is significant because west of Africa there are no navigable rivers until Haiti, Cuba, and the American mainland.

A more circumstantial account of transatlantic contact is available in the *History* of Diodorus of Sicily who lived in the first century B.C.[14] Sicily had important Phoenician cities, and we know from Josephus that the Phoenicians kept voluminous written records. In any case, Diodorus' information is detailed. After describing the islands within the Mediterranean, Diodorus (5:19:1–5) proceeds to tell of a vast "island" in the ocean many days [15] to the west off the coast of Africa. Much of it is mountainous but it is favored also with beautiful plains. Diodorus states that it has navigable rivers (a feature in which the mariners who reported its discovery would be interested). As we have already observed, the only great land mass west of Africa with navigable rivers is America (inclusive of some large islands in the Caribbean). Diodorus mentions that on the "island" were people with well-constructed homes and irrigated groves and gardens. If his information is correct, those inhabitants of America (in Phoenician times) must have been civilized and possessed advanced agriculture and architecture.

In 5:20:1–4 Diodorus explains that the distance of the island from the known world caused it to remain undiscovered until the Phoenicians chanced upon it. "The Phoenicians, who from ancient times on made voyages continually for the purpose of trade, planted many colonies throughout Africa and not a few as well in the western parts of Europe.[16] And since their ventures turned out according to their expectations, they amassed great wealth and tried to voyage beyond the Pillars of Hercules into the sea which men call the ocean." Diodorus goes on to tell how the Phoenicians founded Cadiz (which is on the south coast of Spain, west of Gibraltar; i.e., on the Atlantic Ocean). "The Phoenicians, then, while exploring the coast outside the Pillars (= the Straits of Gibraltar) for the reasons we have stated and while sailing along the shores of Libya (= Africa), were driven by strong winds a great distance out into the ocean. And after being storm-tossed for many days they were carried ashore on the island we mentioned above, and when they observed its felicity and nature they caused it to be known to all men. Consequently the Tyrrhenians (= Etruscans), at the time they were masters of the sea, intended to dispatch a colony to it; but the Carthaginians prevented their doing so, partly lest many inhabitants of Carthage should move there because of the excellence of the island, and partly to have ready in it a place in which to seek refuge against an incalculable turn of fortune, in case some total disaster should overtake Carthage. For it was their thought that, since they were masters of the sea, they would be able to move, households and all, to an island which was unknown to their conquerors."

Once navigation was instituted on the Atlantic, the discovery of America, by accident if not by daring, became inevitable. The winds and currents all favor the sailors' reaching America from the West African shore.

There are many problems in this account. One is the apparent discrepancy between the Phoenicians' first announcing the discovery and later endeavoring to keep it secret. Actually there is nothing unusual about "classifying" information that has already become known. This is the familiar process of "hushing up." There are always many well-known facts in every period of history that are systematically "hushed up" so that people stop discussing them.

If we take Diodorus' account of the "island" at its face value, only the discovery of America can be meant. It is interesting to note how modern writers, who are unprepared for this conclusion, face the evidence. In the Loeb Classical Library edition of Diodorus Siculus (Vol. III, p. 145, footnote 1) apropos of 5:19 describing the island, the editor observes: "The idyllic colours in which the picture of this island in the Atlantic is painted relieve the historian of any concern over its identification, although by some writers it is identified with the largest island of the Madeira group, which, however, has no navigable rivers." If we analyze this footnote, we see that it means we need not concern ourselves with any geographical identification, and that the Atlantic islands off Africa do not satisfy the requirement of navigable rivers. Then commenting on 5:20 (p. 150, footnote 1) the same editor has to admit: "There seems no reason to doubt the statement that Phoenician sailors were actually driven out at some time to islands in the Atlantic, such as Madeira or the Canaries. Cp. R. Hennig, *Historische Zeitschrift,* 139 (1928), 9." In other words, because the outstanding authority (Hennig) on ancient discovery says that Phoenician sailors must have now and then been driven out by storms into the Atlantic, we cannot doubt Diodorus' statement to that effect. However, the editor, after telling us that we are relieved from any need to identify the island, now tells us that it might be Madeira or the Canaries, though they are ruled out because they have no navigable rivers—as he has admitted above. At the price of confusion and egregious inconsistency, he remains unwilling to admit that the island can only be in the Western Hemisphere, simply because academic respectability, at least in his Classics circles, did not allow that possibility in 1939 when his translation was published.

In the second century A.D., Aelian, a Roman author who wrote in Greek, was familiar with the New World described by Theopompus as the only "continent," for it was "infinite," whereas Europe, Asia and Africa were only "islands" surrounded by "Ocean." [17]

The ancient author who best understood the problem as a whole is Strabo who lived in the first centuries B.C. and A.D.[18] His main arguments concerning the wide-ranging navigation of mariners during what we call the second millennium B.C. remain valid after two thousand years.

In his opus called the *Geography,* Strabo states (1:3:2) that he is dealing not with men and times before written records, but with the ancients about whom we have written sources. By the latter, "the ancients will be shown to have made longer journeys, both by land and by sea, than have men of a later time." He reasons that if we consider the exploits of ancient heroes such as Jason, navigational feats were the order of the day. Moreover, the earliest classical author, Homer, depicts not only Odysseus but also Menelaus as undertaking long voyages by sea.

Strabo (1:1:10) realizes that Homer "has inserted things of a mythical nature in his historical and didactic narrative" which is another way of saying that in handling literary (and particularly poetic) documents, we must be critical if we are to extract the kernels of historic truth. He is right in implying that the world reflected in Homer is one in which mariners were sailing the ocean as well as the Mediterranean and its inland extensions such as the Black Sea. The wandering of Odysseus by sea, before he returned to Ithaca after the Trojan War, is not history but it reflects an age of navigation in distant waters not only in the Mediterranean but beyond. For this reason, Henriette

Mertz has undertaken to identify the scenes of his sea exploits as far west as America on the basis of specific details in the Homeric narrative.[19]

Not many generations ago, scholars believed that the Trojan War was a poet's creation without any historic foundation. Schliemann's faith in the historicity of the *Iliad* led to the archeological discovery of ancient Troy. (Now, the actuality of the Trojan War is established, however much Homer's account of it is poetic.) Rightly understood, Strabo (3:2:13) is correct in stating that Homer "also transferred the Odyssey, just as he had already transferred the Iliad, from the domain of historical fact to that of creative art, and to that of mythical invention so familiar to the poets." Strabo (3:2:14) regards the Phoenicians as "the informants of Homer, and these people (i.e., the Phoenicians) occupied the best of Iberia and Libya before the age of Homer, and continued to be masters of those regions until the Romans broke up their empire."

According to Strabo (1:3:2) "the Phoenicians a short time after the Trojan War explored the reigons beyond the Pillars of Hercules and founded cities both there and in the central parts of the Libyan seaboard." A knowledge of the ocean surrounding all the known continents underlies the Homeric concept of geography; and Strabo attributes such knowledge to ancient mariners such as the Phoenicians.

In 1:1:8 Strabo makes the interesting observation that "the inhabited world is an island; for wherever it has been possible for man to reach the limits of the earth, sea has been found, and this sea we call 'Oceanus.' " (This passage incidentally makes it clear that "island" in Greek could be applied to a land mass of continental size.)

This concept of the inhabited earth washed on all sides by "Oceanus" is attributed to Homer by Strabo (1:1:3) because Homer "makes the sun to rise out of Oceanus and to set in Oceanus; and he refers in the same way to the stars." Moreover (1:1:7) "in the story of the arms of Achilles, Homer places Oceanus in a circle round the outer edge of the Shield of Achilles" to indicate that the land is encircled by water. Strabo notes (in the same section) other proofs that Homer knew of the ocean. Thus Homer refers to tide, which characterizes the oceans but not to any great extent inland seas such as the Mediterranean.

The process of long-range navigation must precede the Phoenicians, if we define them (as historians often do, implicitly or explicitly) as entering the stage of history around 1200 B.C. Actually the Minoans, who dominated Crete and the Aegean in the Middle Bronze Age (2000–1600 B.C.) and gradually lost their grip during the Late Bronze Age (1600–1200 B.C.), were related to the "Phoenicians" linguistically [20] and as regards their nautical way of life. Strabo (1:3:2) is among the Greek authors who know of the "thalassocracy" of Minos. The fact that the classical Greeks, who had already learned to live by and on the sea, remembered the Minoans as "thalassocrats" (i.e., sea-lords) indicates, as Strabo correctly implies, the superiority of the Minoans over the classical Greeks and Romans in the art of seafaring.

The testimony of Strabo may be summed up thus: before the continental concept of the classical world, there was a maritime view of the world based on the oceanic voyages of ancients such as the Minoans and Phoenicians in the Bronze and Early Iron ages. By Roman times the geographical horizons of mankind were shrinking back to the continental view, which persisted to the time of Columbus.[21]

We may now turn to the most discussed and controversial of all ancient sources bearing on the New World: Plato's Atlantis. Plato lived in the fourth century B.C. In his *Timaeus,* Plato tells of Atlantis: a vast island west of the Pillars of Hercules, larger than Africa and Asia combined, about which Solon, while visiting the Nile Delta, had learned from an Egyptian priest. (In his *Critias,* Plato has more to say about the description and institutions of Atlantis.) [22] Because of its presence voyagers could cross the Atlantic Ocean: from Europe or Africa to Atlantis, thence westward to other islands and finally to a real continent.[23] The kings of Atlantis forged an empire embracing Atlantis, many islands, part of that continent in the West, North Africa up to Egypt, and Europe up to Etruria. From their Mediterranean positions they threatened the Levant, which the Greeks (especially the Athenians) saved. Subsequently a sudden cataclysm of earthquakes sank Atlantis so that the span of water between the Pillars of Hercules and the islands and continent in the west was too great for ships to cross. Thus were contacts broken between what we call today the Eastern and Western Hemispheres.

Obviously the account of Atlantis in the *Timaeus* is not factual history in the ordinary sense of the word. The glorification of Athens as the savior of Greece and the entire Levant against the Atlantids is evoked by pride in an illustrious city. Geologically, strange and cataclysmic changes have taken place, and there are some writers who maintain that the Azores, Madeira, the Canaries and Cape Verde Islands are the peaks of Atlantis that alone remain of a vast island. Other oceanographers, whom I have consulted, assure me that the Atlantis legend is geologically impossible. I am not competent to make an independent judgment on the Atlantis question. Nevertheless something should be said about the legendary aspects of disappearing islands, before we try to extract any history from the Atlantis legend.

Merchant mariners like the Phoenicians cultivated a policy of keeping their sources of wealth secret. Their attitude is exemplified in Strabo's narrative (3:5:11) of a Phoenician captain trading with the Cassiterides ("The Tin Islands"). A Roman ship trailed him, intending to discover the Phoenicians' source of supply. But the Phoenician captain lured the Roman ship into shoal waters, so that both vessels were wrecked. The Phoenician captain, however, escaped and received from the State the value of his cargo. He had served his people well, and kept their secret from their Roman competitors.

Against this background we see a motive for inventing stories about islands that have sunk in the sea. The oldest tale of this kind is the Middle Egyptian tale of the Shipwrecked Sailor, composed during the first half of the second millennium b.c. We shall consider that text in a later chapter. Here suffice it to note the earliest parallel in classical Greek literature: the story of the Land of the Phaeacians in the Odyssey. Odysseus is shipwrecked in that wondrous land, from which he returns to his home laden with gifts. But there is no use looking for Phaeacia because, as the text tells us, it has been cut off from the rest of the world by a cataclysm.[24]

Several historic problems are raised by the Atlantis legend. Minoan civilization confronts us with characteristics very different from the rest of the Near East where the written sources start over a thousand years before the rise of the Minoans, and the archeological sources much earlier.

The Minoans display a sense of movement unknown among the earlier Mesopotamians and Egyptians whose art is rather static. The Mi-

Minoan Snake Goddess of ivory trimmed with gold. COURTESY,
MUSEUM OF FINE ARTS, BOSTON

noan style of dress and coiffure is distinctive, with feathered headdresses unmistakably like those in the New World. More specific is the
evidence of script. The Minoan hieroglyphs and syllabary are distinctive vis-à-vis the Egyptian and Mesopotamian systems of writing; contacts between the Minoan and other Old World systems are secondary
or accretional. What is striking is the series of epigraphical links between the scripts of the New World and those of the Minoan and Phoenician navigators of the Mediterranean (about which we shall have
more to say). To state that everything started in the Aegean and
moved westward is a one-sided and unnatural approach. The appeal of
Atlantis is precisely the intermediate location of the legendary island,
linking the Old and New Worlds. But we do not really need Atlantis,
and because of the nebulous status of Atlantis speculations, we shall
be well advised in not attaching any weight to it until it is clarified one
way or the other. It is becoming abundantly clear that there was an
important element in the fabric of the Bronze Age Mediterranean: an
international network of merchant mariners organized in guilds. We
know of them from texts such as the Ugaritic tablets (1400–1200
B.C.). Thalassocrats cannot be pinned down to any special land area.
They control islands and ports from which they exploit whatever continental districts are necessary for raw materials. They do not try to
dominate whole continents for the sake of creating a land empire.
Scripts related in form to the Minoan syllabary and/or the Phoenician
alphabet have been found all over the Mediterranean from Western
Asia to Spain and in America.[25]

We must begin to reckon with "Sea Peoples" as well as "Land Peoples." Assyro-Babylonians hailed from Mesopotamia, the Medes and
the Persians from Iran, the Egyptians from the Nile Valley, and so
forth. But there were also Sea People such as the Minoans and Phoenicians, to whom we are indebted for much of our civilization including
the alphabet.

In the Bronze Age the great network of merchant mariners was not
limited to the Mediterranean or other inland seas. It was oceanic and
intercontinental.

Our problem is psychological. Like the classical Greeks and Romans, and like the Europeans before the fifteenth century A.D., our
concept of history is continental rather than maritime. This is all right

The goddess Hathor embracing the Pharaoh Mycerinus. On the left is Nome goddess. Giza (ca. twenty-fifth century B.C.*).*
COURTESY, MUSEUM OF FINE ARTS, BOSTON

Persian warrior from Persepolis (ca. 500 B.C.*).* COURTESY,
MUSEUM OF FINE ARTS, BOSTON

in dealing with periods where the outlook was continental, such as eras of conquest by the Assyrians, Persians, Macedonians, Romans, and so on. But it is quite mistaken when we apply it (albeit subconsciously) to the Middle and Late Bronze ages, and to the periods of Phoenician enterprise in the Early Iron Age.

Now that we have reached the moon and are planning to set foot on other planets, it should not be too much for us to take in our stride the historic role of merchant mariners who sailed the Seven Seas and have left their texts and monuments as testimony.

By the same token, the reports in Old World literature concerning the New World in antiquity mean that we have potential clues for deciphering the inscriptions of the New World. The Greek classics are now of importance for unlocking the mysteries of ancient America, even as they have been for providing opening wedges in the decipherments of the forgotten scripts of the Old World.

To sum up: Greek classics independently and repeatedly attest transatlantic contacts between the Mediterranean and America.

Chapter III

THE PLUMED SERPENT

T H E T R E N D of archeology has been to confirm tradition against modern theories. For example, Homeric epic was written off historically and relegated to the realm of foundationless legend and myth. Heinrich Schliemann, an amateur with a love for and faith in the Iliad, went to Troy and Mycenae, and through his excavations laid the foundation for restoring the Mycenaean era to its rightful place in history. This does not mean that the verbatim declarations attributed in hexameter to Agamemnon or Nestor are their actual speeches as a tape recorder would have recorded them, nor that the mortal Peleus impregnated the goddess Thetis with Achilles, nor that the sun was made to stand still so that the Achaeans had the extra daylight hours they needed to score a victory, nor that the corpse of Hector was miraculously exempted from decomposition. Until we understand the nature of ancient East Mediterranean myth, legend, epic poetry, religion and psychology, we are unprepared to deal with the historic aspects of Homeric, Biblical, Ugaritic and other ancient literatures.

Drinking vessels, weapons, technologies, etc., as reflected in the Homeric text, are frequently correct in that they reflect the material culture of the Aegean as the Bronze Age was giving way to the Iron Age.[26] That the divine, personal and place names are not anachronistic is clear from the excavations and Linear B tablets. That the Trojan War did take place—in spite of many debatable aspects of it—is no longer questioned.

The same is true of the native American traditions, which we must evaluate as traditions before we can hope to extract from them their historic elements. The Aztecs have a tradition that the arts of civilization were brought to America by a bearded white personage named Quetzalcoatl, "The Plumed Serpent." He came from the east by boat, which can only mean across the Atlantic. So firm was their faith in him, that it played into the hands of Cortés. The Aztecs were expecting Quetzalcoatl to return in A.D. 1519—by sheer coincidence the very year that Cortés arrived. By the time the Aztecs realized that Cortés was no beneficent being, but a ruthless conqueror, it was too late.

The Maya have the same tradition about the bearded white being who came from the east bringing the blessings of civilization. They call him in their own language Kukulcan which means The Plumed Serpent. Thus the tradition is the same, but the name is different in sound though identical in meaning. The Inca cherish the same tradition though they call him Viracocha. And the coastal Indians of Brazil tell of the same type of being (though he "walked on water") [27] but call him Sume.

These traditions—which are really variants of the same persistent tradition—point to white people with beards, who crossed the Atlantic and made fundamental contributions to the diffusion of culture from the Mediterranean and Europe to Mesoamerica and some areas in the northern half of South America, as well as (for reasons we shall review later) parts of the southern half of North America.

In legend and myth a personage can be treated in the form of his epithets. Thus the U.S.A. can be depicted as the slender, bearded "Uncle Sam" wearing a red, white and blue costume; while "John Bull" is an entirely different personage who we know stands for England. In a political cartoon, it is assumed that the public knows an elephant stands for the Republican Party, while a donkey represents the Democratic Party. In pre-Columbian art, the Plumed Serpent represented the deified bearded white men who had brought civilization from the east.

The classical Old World has something to say about bearded white men who are at the same time plumed serpents. A pediment from the Athenian acropolis portrays on one side three plumed serpents, each with the head of a bearded man. This embodies the essential traits—

The Bearded Human Headed Feathered Serpents (from a pediment of an archaic temple on the Athenian Acropolis).

Detail showing the feathers the Bearded Human Headed Serpents (from a pediment of an archaic temple on the Athenian Acropolis).

at two levels—of the American iconography. First, we are dealing with a bearded white man from the Mediterranean; second, he is at the same time a feathered serpent. There are too many details involved to be attributed to accident. The diffusion of ideas from the Mediterranean to Mesoamerica explains the facts more reasonably than a psychological approach implying that it is so natural for men to conceive of bearded white men who are at the same time feathered serpents, that the same combination naturally developed independently at the ends of the earth in isolation.

Parts of the Serpent tradition appear elsewhere in ancient records. In Genesis 3:1, the Serpent is the cleverest of all creatures. Although he incited mankind to rebel against God's orders, he is represented as giving Eve correct information, opening the eyes of mankind to universal knowledge and enabling the human race to embark on the arts of civilization, starting with agriculture. A price had of course to be paid: the loss of an existence (one can hardly call it a life) of indolence in a static paradise. The Serpent talks in the language of men, and Church art, which often depicts the Serpent with a human head, may well represent the concept of the early Hebrews correctly. As members of the East Mediterranean community of nations, the Hebrews may have envisaged the Serpent much as the Athenians who expressed themselves pictorially on the Acropolis pediment.

Civilization is stimulated by the interaction of peoples; much of the stimulation came by sea. This is reflected in the tradition of Quetzalcoatl who brought the arts of civilization (from agriculture to metallurgy) across the Atlantic to Mesoamerica. There is a parallel in Mesopotamia.

In the third century B.C. (around 280) a Babylonian priest named Berossus wrote in Greek an account of his native Mesopotamian culture entitled *Babyloniaca*. In it he ascribes all the arts and sciences to a primeval being, half-man half-fish, named Oannes, who came out of the sea (i.e., the Persian Gulf) and taught man everything there is to know. Since then nothing new has been learned though much has been forgotten. We know that Sumerian civilization was established from the outside, because Sumer (i.e., southern Iraq) does not produce the metals and stones without which Sumerian civilization is unthinkable. Sumer excelled in the arts of the lapidary, coppersmith, goldsmith and silversmith. The alluvial soil of Sumer is pure river silt without any minerals. The materials used by the Sumerians from the beginning of their civilization came from many directions and from great distances. For example, the lapis lazuli was imported from Afghanistan. When archeologists found Sumerian-type clay tablets in Romanian Transylvania from about 2700 B.C.[28] (the oldest known inscriptions from Europe!), many a savant was completely mystified. Actually there is no mystery about it. Transylvania is full of minerals, including gold, which the Sumerians needed to get because there was none in Sumer. Sumerian civilization cannot be explained as a product of agricultural Sumer, whereby a nation of farmers lifted themselves by their bootstraps to excel in the arts of the gem cutter and metallurgist which required minerals from the ends of the known world. On the contrary, there is every reason to envisage the prehistoric Sumerians as masters of a network of bases spread over a wide area, with a central body that got a foothold in Babylonia while continuing to operate its far-flung network. We need not be surprised that one base was at Tartaria, near Cluj, in Romanian Transylvania. That some of the Sumerians came by sea is a foregone conclusion, because we know of early contacts between Sumer and the Indus Valley culture. Contact by ship is much easier than overland between the two areas. Hence Oannes—the source of all civilization—emerges from the Sea, and the Sumerian sea god Enki is the divine repository of wisdom and knowledge. We should have no difficulty understanding such concepts, for did not the seeds of our modern so-called Western civilization come to the shores of the U.S.A. by sea from Europe?

There is an Egyptian novelette that bears on the problem of the talking bearded serpent. In ancient Mexico, Quetzalcoatl is identified with the ruler. In fact Montezuma still wore the feathered crown of Quetzalcoatl, and was regarded as the Plumed Serpent incarnate, when Cortés came. This sort of imagery is not uncommon. In Egypt the Pharaoh was the falcon god, Horus, incarnate. Any Egyptian seeing the Falcon in art knew when it represented the Pharaoh. And in Egyptian literature, the Pharaoh could be referred to as "The Falcon." Our Egyptian novelette, called The Shipwrecked Sailor,[29] deals with a far-off wondrous island whose ruler was a bearded, talking serpent, even as Quetzalcoatl, the human ruler, was at the same time a bearded, talk-

Head of Gudea, Sumerian ruler of Lagash (ca. 2000 B.C.*). Gudea tells how he secured minerals from different parts of the Old World for his building program.* COURTESY, MUSEUM OF FINE ARTS, BOSTON

ing serpent. The text, composed in the Middle Egyptian language, was probably written during the Twelfth Dynasty during the first quarter of the second millennium B.C. It is therefore a source bearing on our problem, written long before we can speak of Greek, Hebrew or even of Ugaritic literatures. It comes from the Middle Bronze Age (2000–1600 B.C.), while "The Megalithic Mariners" (Chapter IV) were sailing the seas to leave a trail of megalithic monuments from the Mediterranean out into the Atlantic: for their greatest achievement is at Stonehenge in England.

We shall translate the text with a running commentary.

"The noble courtier said: 'Let your heart be hale, O captain!' " The captain has just returned from a distant merchant marine mission and is about to report to the Pharaoh. A well-meaning courtier is trying to prepare the captain for facing the anxieties of the situation by reminding him of his safe return for which he should be thankful.

"We have reached the Residence (where the Pharaoh is), the mallet has been seized and the mooring stake driven in and the prow rope fastened on land. Give praise and adore God, for every man is hugging his fellow. Our crew has come back safely, without loss of our personnel. We have reached Wawat and Senmut. We have returned in peace and reached our land."

The courtier now proceeds to tell his own story to cheer up the captain, who is understandably nervous about the impression he may make before the august Pharaoh.

"Listen to me, O captain! I am devoid of exaggeration. Wash yourself, put water on your fingers.[30] Then you will answer when you are addressed; you will speak with poise to the Pharaoh, answering without faltering. The mouth of a man can save him; his words can get indulgence for him. But you will do according to the dictates of your heart. It is tiresome talking (this way) to you. I'm going to tell you something similar that happened to myself. I was going to the mines of the Sovereign."

It is important to note that the main purpose of these marine expeditions was to get minerals. No place was too far—nor the way to it too arduous—if its metals and stones were valuable enough for the king, who sponsored all his nation's foreign enterprises. (There was

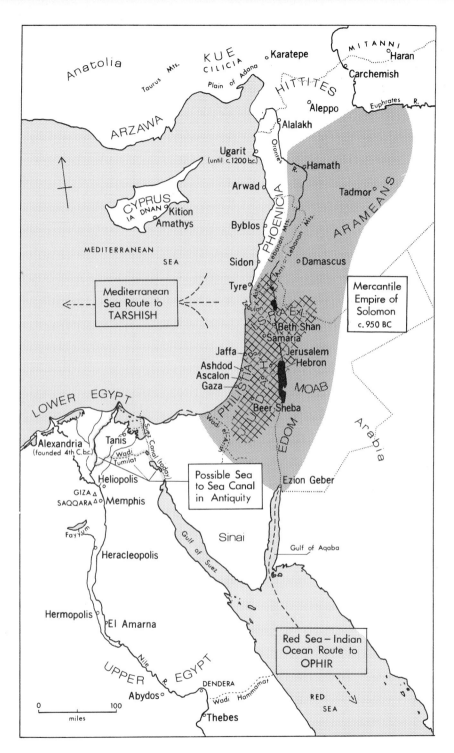

EAST MEDITERRANEAN

no private enterprise throughout antiquity in the sense that it now exists in modern capitalistic society.)

"I went down to the sea in a ship, a hundred and twenty cubits long, and forty wide."

The ship is by ancient standards large (about one hundred and eighty feet long, and sixty feet wide), but it must reflect realistically the dimensions of big oceangoing ships used by the Egyptians. The Tale of the Shipwrecked Sailor is fiction, but it aims at convincing the reader that it is "in this world" and not out of it. A modern novel describing Queen Elizabeth's limousine would refer not to a car of compact or standard dimensions, but to an oversize yet real automobile such as a Rolls-Royce. While the Shipwrecked Sailor's vessel may seem puny compared with our oceangoing liners, it was far bigger than Columbus's *Nina, Pinta* or *Santa Maria*. The same may be said of the larger cargo ships attested in administrative tablets from Ugarit of the Late Bronze Age, where the evidence is factual, and devoid of any fictional aspects.

"A crew of a hundred and twenty, the pick of Egypt, manned it. They had seen the heavens and seen the earth. Their heart was braver than lions."

First-class personnel was selected. These mariners were not ordinary draftees or unqualified volunteers. They were literally selectees, for only the best mariners of Egypt were suitable on such an important and difficult mission for the Pharaoh. None of these men were tyros; they were familiar with "heaven and earth" which means everywhere and everything. Such expressions of totality made by combining a pair of antonyms are common. This particular one is found in Genesis 1:1 for "—God created the heavens and the earth" means "—God created the universe (everything, everywhere)." "Heavens," to be sure, meant something to the mariners that it needn't signify to us, because they found their way on the high seas largely through celestial navigation. Note that the bravery of the mariners is singled out, for their way of life required intrepid men.

"They could predict a storm ere it came; a hurricane ere it happened."

Mariners had to be skilled in the art of weather prediction, and this crew was.

"A storm arose while we were at sea before we could reach land, driven by the wind, [which] kept making wave[s] of eight cubits. A beam of wood hit me; the ship foundered. Of those who were on it, not one was saved. Then I was cast by a wave of the sea on an island. I spent three days alone with my heart as my (only) companion. I lay down in an arbor of wood, embracing the shade. I found figs and grapes there, and all sorts of excellent vegetables. *K'w* fruit was there together with *nqwt* fruit and cucumbers like those cultivated. Fish there were together with birds. There is nothing that was not in its midst. Then I satisfied myself and put [the rest] on the ground for it was too much for my two hands. I carved a wooden drill, produced a fire, and made a burnt offering to the gods."

Though the crew had predicted the storm, it came upon them too suddenly for finding a haven. The narrator was the sole survivor and was washed ashore on an island of untold abundance: a distant paradise abounding in the finest edible plants, fish and fowl. The Shipwrecked Sailor eats to satiety and makes a burnt offering of the surplus to the gods. Ancient man served the gods in his own traditional way wherever he went, which is why cultic practices and religious ideas spread so widely as a result of international land and sea travel.

"Then I heard a noise [like] thunder that I fancied was a [tidal] wave of the sea. Trees were breaking, earth was quaking. When I uncovered my face, I found it was a serpent coming, thirty cubits long. His beard was over two cubits long. His body was plated with gold, his eyebrows were of pure lapis lazuli."

The wondrous serpent, who rules the island, is bearded, like Quetzalcoatl, who is also represented as a bearded serpent. Just as the falcon of Horus can represent the Pharaoh (for every Pharaoh was regarded as Horus incarnate), the bearded serpent can represent the king of the far-off island. We indulge (as noted above) in this kind of symbolism much as the ancients; a lion can represent Britain; a lion holding a sword and with a sunburst over his back represents Iran; another style of lion stands for the Emperor of Ethiopia; a goat represents the U.S. Naval Academy; a mule, the Army Academy; a donkey, the Democratic Party; an elephant, the Republican Party. Similarly, the bearded serpent represents the greater-than-lifesize king of the island in this Egyptian text, much as it represents the greater-than-lifesize figure of

Quetzalcoatl who is both king and god. The serpent has no plumes in our text. Parallels—even those that are firmly established as historical —are never identical. If we did not know the history of Christianity, an Eastern Orthodox church in the Near East would appear unrelated to a typical Protestant church in a Vermont village. Transmission always means change, and it is up to us to detect the transmitted factors as well as the new features.

The covering of the body with gold, and the lapis-lazuli eyebrows go hand in hand with Egyptian (and other ancient) sculpture which included statues overlaid with gold and inlaid lapis-lazuli eyebrows. Texts and art are parallel expressions of human culture; men can express themselves verbally or artistically. This is why texts may explain features of the art; and why, by the same token, art may clear up obscurities in the texts. To get back to the story:

"He coiled himself forward, opening his mouth to me, while I was on my belly in his presence. He said to me: 'Who brought you? Who brought you, Little One? If you delay in telling me who brought you to this island, I'll make you find yourself turned to ashes—become what can no longer be seen.' [I answered:] 'You speak to me but I cannot hear it. While I am in your [august] presence, I don't know who I am.' Then he put me in his mouth, carrying me off to his favorite lair. He set me down without hurting me. I was intact without anything torn from me. He opened his mouth to me while I was on my belly in his presence. Then he said to me: 'Who brought you? Who brought you, Little One? Who brought you to this island of the sea whose borders are surrounded by water?' Then I answered him with my arms folded in his presence, and said to him: 'I was going down to the mines on a mission of the Sovereign in a ship a hundred and twenty cubits long and forty cubits wide. A crew of a hundred and twenty were on it, the pick of Egypt. They had seen the heavens, and seen the earth. Their heart was braver than lions. They could predict a storm ere it came; a hurricane ere it happened. Every one was stouter of heart and stronger of arm than his fellow. There wasn't a misfit among them. A storm arose while we were at sea before we could reach land, driven by the wind. It redoubled with an eight-cubit wave. A beam of wood hit me; the ship foundered. None of those in it were saved but me

Ptah-Kenuwy and his wife. This pair of statues illustrates the custom of ceremonially reddening men and whitening (or alternatively yellowing) women. The custom was practiced by the Egyptians, Hebrews, Ugaritians, Greeks, Etruscans and other Mediterranean people. The ceremonial reddening among American Indian men is to be compared. COURTESY, MUSEUM OF FINE ARTS, BOSTON

alone. Here I am at your side. I have been brought to this island by a wave of the sea.' He said to me: 'Don't fear! Don't fear, Little One! Strengthen your countenance for you have reached me. Behold, God has destined you to live. He has brought you to this island of Ka, in whose midst nothing is lacking; it is full of all good things. Behold you will spend month after month here till you complete four months in the midst of this island, when a ship will come from the [Pharaoh's] Residence. You know the crew on it and you will go with them to the Residence and die in your native city. How nice it is to tell what one has experienced after the bitter things have passed! I shall tell you something similar that happened on this island.' "

The Shipwrecked Sailor's recapitulation of his story with variations, though in essentially the same words as already narrated, is a common stylistic feature in ancient Egyptian, Semitic and classical literatures. The same holds for what comes next: a *dramatis persona* tells his life story to a visitor. Also we have a story within a story, within a story: a stylistic feature common enough in ancient Near East and other literatures.[31]

" 'I used to be in it with my brethren, my children among them; we totaled seventy-three serpents, children together with brethren; I do not mention to you a little daughter brought to me in consequence of a prayer. Then a star fell and these (serpents) went forth in the flame it produced. It chanced I was not with them when they were burned. I was not among them [but] I just about died for them, when I found them as one corpse. If you are brave, control your heart, and you will fill your embrace with your children and kiss your wife and see your house. That is better than anything. You will reach the [Pharaoh's] Residence and be in it in the midst of your brethren.' "

The happy outcome predicted by the serpent is the homecoming. This is of course a natural desire that is too common to require comment. However, it is worth noting that the ancient mariners were normally on missions for the homeland under the sponsorship of their own king. They were not as a rule colonists seeking new homes and a new life overseas. This will explain to a great extent the nature of the Old World impact on ancient Mesoamerica. Quetzalcoatl comes by ship, makes a cultural and technological impression in Mexico, leaves by ship, and is expected to return. He is an important visitor who makes a deep impression; he may return periodically but is not a colonizer.

The Shipwrecked Sailor continues:

"Extended on my belly and touching the ground in his presence, I said to him: 'I shall declare your might to the Sovereign and cause him to know your greatness. I shall have the finest spices brought to you, and temple incense wherewith every god is gratified. I shall tell what happened and what I have seen of his (i.e., Your Majesty's) power. God shall be praised for you in the city, before the magistrates of the entire land. I shall slay oxen for you as a burnt offering and sacrifice fowl for you. I shall have ships brought to you laden with all the luxuries of Egypt as is done for a god who loves men in a distant land which men do not know.' "

Side by side, we find polytheism and monotheism, without any concern for what the modern philosophical mind must rule out as inconsistency. The same situation is reflected time and again in the Bible, let alone in other ancient literatures. This flexible attitude facilitated the spread of religious ideas and practices, ranging from the diffusion of lofty monotheistic universalism to the most barbaric rites including human sacrifice. The influence of the Old World on the New is more easily documented than the converse, as of now; but we may be sure that the cultural influence is here, as always, a two-way street (though the influence in one direction may outweigh that in the other direction).

"Then he laughed at me as the things said were as folly in his mind. So he said to me: 'You have no abundance of myrrh and every fine spice and incense. But I am the ruler of Punt. I've got the myrrh in it, and that spice you said you'd bring is plentiful on this island. It will happen that when you depart from this place, this island will never be seen again, for it will become water.' "

The island, like all the lands worth sailing to, is rich in resources. This island is represented as being in the Red Sea or adjacent parts of the Indian Ocean, for its ruler claims to rule Punt, which must be along the east coast of Africa, around Somaliland. We are reviewing this text not because it deals with the New World (for it patently does not) but to show the attitudes toward seaborne missions. The disappearance of the island shows that the sunken island motif was common long before Plato's Atlantis. Indeed Plato tells us that Solon heard about Atlantis from an Egyptian priest who said that it had happened of old: nine thousand years earlier!

"Then the ship did arrive as he had foretold. I went and set myself on a high tree and recognized those who were in it. So I betook myself to report it but I found he already knew it. Then he said to me: 'Safely, safely, Little One, back to your home! You will see your children. Make my name blessed in your city. This is what you owe me.'

"Then I prostrated myself on my belly with my arms folded in his presence. Thereupon he gave me a load of myrrh and assorted fine spices, mascara, giraffe tails, a great bundle of incense, elephant tusks, hounds, monkeys, apes [32] and every fine luxury. I loaded it on that boat, prostrated myself on my belly to praise God for him. Whereupon he said to me: 'Behold you will reach the [Pharaoh's] Residence in two months. You will embrace your children, flourish in the Residence till you are buried there.'"

Burial on one's native soil was of prime importance not only for universally sentimental reasons, but specifically because it was felt that only at home could the deceased be cared for by his own people and his own gods. The community was viewed as consisting of the local population—living and dead—along with their local gods. With no family and gods to look after the dead, the latter could only have a wretched afterlife without even the offerings of food and water to provide minimum comfort. Indeed stories like The Shipwrecked Sailor are known to us only from scrolls placed in tombs to provide the deceased with good reading matter for entertainment in the afterlife. The cult of the dead included an assortment of amenities over and above absolute necessities such as food and drink. To us this may seem a make-believe world; to the Egyptians it was so real that it was necessary for making life on earth worthwhile. [33] This alone induced Egyptian mariners to return to their native cities along the Nile and served as a deterrent to permanent migration. The implication is that their art of navigation included the capability of finding their way back from the most distant ports they visited.

"Then I went down to the shore where that ship was and called to the personnel who were on that ship. On the shore I gave praise to the lord of this island; those on the ship did likewise. We voyaged north-ward to the Residence of the Sovereign."

The voyage was northward, and so the last lap was down the Nile. The omission of any land travel separating the sea and river travel suggests that the whole trip was made aboard the same boat through the canal that joined the Nile to the Red Sea [34] so that in effect boats from the East could not only navigate to the Nile, but through it also to the Mediterranean millennia before the Suez Canal was opened in A.D. 1869.

"We reached the Residence in two months, in accordance with all he had said. I entered into the presence of the Sovereign and presented him with the tribute I had brought from the midst of that island. There-upon he praised God for me in front of the grandees of the entire land. I was then made a retainer, in charge of two hundred men and women. Look at me, [who] reached the Land, after all I have seen and experi-enced! So listen to my words, for it is good to listen to people!"

Here end the words of the Shipwrecked Sailor, whose tale, though it occupies nearly the entire scroll, is technically the story within a story to inspire good cheer in the captain who is nervous at the pros-pect of reporting to the Pharaoh. The captain's cryptic reply, which apparently means someone else's life story with a glib happy ending, is of little comfort when we are faced with an imminent crisis:

"Then he [the captain] said to me [the Shipwrecked Sailor]: 'Don't be so superior, my friend! Who gives water to a bird he will slaughter at dawn on the morrow?' "

The simile implies that cheering up a doomed man is like wasting water on a bird just before killing it. The colophon tells the name of the scribe who copied the story from a master copy:

"It has come, from its beginning to its end, as found in writing. The scribe, skilled of hand, ᶜA-Amon ["Amon is Great"] the son of Ameny, may he live, prosper and be healthy!"

In this chapter we have endeavored to trace the Plumed Serpent back to Old World antiquity. The Serpent King is very ancient in Egypt. In fact, a Pharaoh of the First Dynasty (early in the third mil-lennium B.C.) whose name is indicated by a snake glyph used to be called the Serpent King. Later Egyptologists pronounced his name Jet;

Sitting Figure from Monte Albán (Mexico). The pose recalls the common Egyptian posture characteristic of scribes. Moreover the tiara and emblems remind one of Egyptian headdresses and hieroglyphs. Yet the validity of such resemblances depends on the identity in detail, which requires further investigation. COURTESY, THE CLEVELAND MUSEUM OF ART

now they prefer to call him Waji. In The Shipwrecked Sailor, the Serpent King is bearded as in the Mesoamerican tradition. On the Athenian Acropolis we find the mythological deified serpents, not only bearded but actually plumed as well, combining the human and serpentine forms like Quetzalcoatl, who was envisaged as a bearded, deified Caucasian and simultaneously as a bearded Plumed Serpent.

Chapter IV

MEGALITHS
AND MARINERS

I N L I F E , T H O U G H T and work, we may be frustrated not only by poverty but also by superabundance. The latter is what the French so aptly describe as *embarras de richesses* ("the encumbrance of wealth"). The problem of links between the Old and New Worlds in antiquity is complicated not so much by dearth of evidence as by the worldwide spread of so much evidence spanning millennia. To cite only a few of the many varied examples: (1) we know that in the Early Stone Age about 30,000 years ago, waves of primitive Mongoloids came to America across what is now the Bering Strait; that (2) around five millennia ago, in the Jomon period, pottery from Japan appeared in Ecuador; that (3) a Roman sculptured head of about A.D. 200 was excavated, professionally, in stratified remains in Mexico;[35] that (4) off the coast of Venezuela was discovered a hoard of Mediterranean coins with so many duplicates that it cannot well be a numismatist's collection but rather a supply of cash. Nearly all the coins are Roman, from the reign of Augustus to the fourth century A.D.; two of the coins, however, are Arabic of the eighth century A.D. It is the latter that give us the *terminus a quo* (i.e., time after which) of the collection as a whole (which cannot be earlier than the latest coins in the collection). Roman coins continued in use as currency into medieval times. A Moorish ship, perhaps from Spain or North Africa, seems to have crossed the Atlantic around A.D. 800.[36] (5) The Coimbra Map of A.D. 1424 shows parts of North America.[37]

Roman head (of ca. A.D. *200) excavated in pyramid at Calixtlahuaca, Mexico.*

Accordingly, we cannot speak of one era, nor of a single group of mankind who came from the Old World to the New, across the Atlantic or Pacific in pre-Columbian antiquity. The traffic in some periods was more active, in others it was quiescent, but the phenomenon took place in depth over the millennia. Now and then, ships were unintentionally carried by wind and current across the ocean, but most of the traffic was planned and should be viewed as part of sustained two-way communication.

This chapter emphasizes only one of the many important aspects of the problem: the megalithic structures erected by seafaring people from the Mediterranean out into the Atlantic, culminating in Stonehenge.[38] The origins of their constructions may possibly go back to Neolithic times, but in any case reached their apogee in the mid-second millennium B.C.

To place the subject in depth, we turn to the maps of Piri Reis which were rediscovered in 1929 in the old Imperial Palace in Istanbul. The principal map was painted on parchment in 1513 by the Turkish Admiral Piri (his title "Reis" means "Chief" or, in this context, "Admiral"). Piri Reis tells us in his writings that the map embodies ancient sources, some of which came via the great library at Alexandria, which was destroyed by the Arab conquerors in the seventh century A.D. There are features of the map which must antedate Columbus' discovery of America in 1492: notably, the essentially correct east coastline of South America in its right longitudinal relationship with the Atlantic coast of the Old World.

The source material, set in its comparative and historic framework, is presented by Charles H. Hapgood in his *Maps of the Ancient Sea Kings* (Chilton, Philadelphia, 1966). Hapgood notes that neither in the Age of Columbus, nor till the mid-eighteenth century A.D., did the Europeans know of any technique for determining longitude accurately—however developed their methods of fixing latitude were. This is clear from Hapgood's review of the maps of the world made not only in the sixteenth and seventeenth centuries A.D., but also the known maps of classical antiquity such as those associated with Ptolemy, and the verbal testimony of classical geographers. Hapgood's inference that there was a preclassical science of navigation and cartography eclipsing anything of the kind from the Iron Age down to the century of the American and French revolutions cannot be brushed aside as

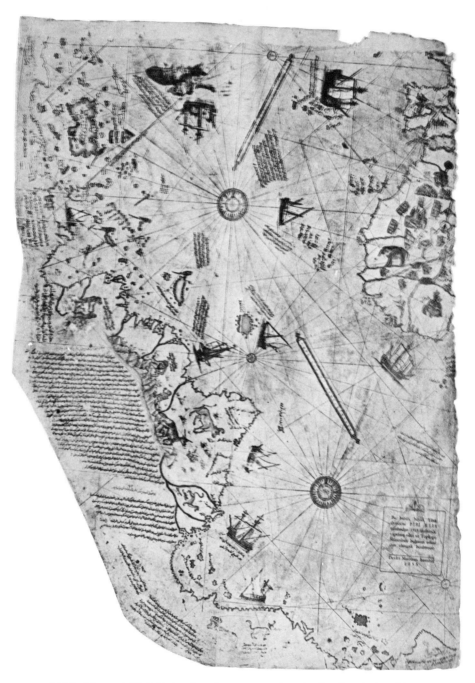

1513 Map of Piri Reis showing correct longitudinal relationship between the Atlantic coast of South America and the Old World.

THE PIRI REIS MAP OF 1513

IN ALL THE WORLD THERE IS NO OTHER
MAP LIKE THIS MAP—PIRI REIS

Key to the Piri Reis Map of 1513.

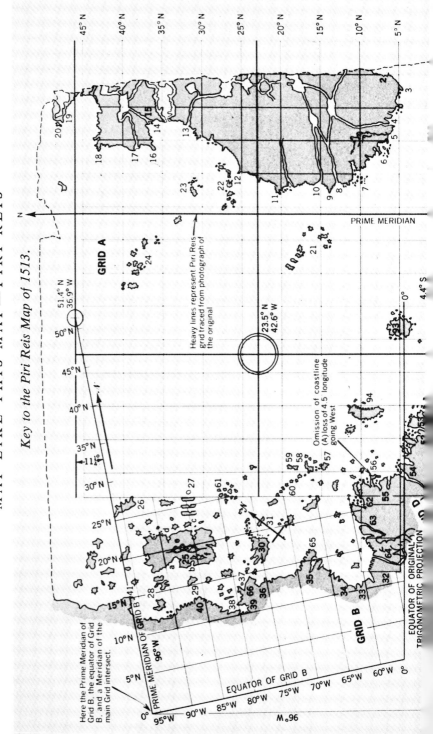

jection based on the pole (Fig. 17).

The latitudes, however, have been modified, (a) by a shift of the whole geography of both sides of the Atlantic about 4.4° northward, apparently on the assumption that the horizontal line through Point III of the portolan design was supposed to be the equator; and (b) by the apparently arbitrary increase in the distance between the parallels, a device to take account of the curvature of the earth that has been attributed to Ptolemy (Note 9). These changes were no doubt the work of later geographers.

The northward shift of the geography of the main grid had the effect of pushing the geography of Grid B westward about 4°, thus increasing the longitude errors of that part of the map.

Grid B is determined both as to latitude and longitude by the trigonometry of the projection based on the main grid. It may be considered as a part of the main grid that has been swung through an arc of about 78¾ degrees. Both the prime meridian and the equator of Grid B can be considered extensions of the lines of Grid A.

For a list of the numbered geographical points, see below. For a list of the numbered geographical points with comparative tables of their latitudes and longitudes, see Table 1.

Grids C and D represent errors in compilation, Grid C having an error in scale, and Grid D being unrelated to the trigonometric projection.

Figures in brackets represent latitude adjusted for omissions of part of the South American Coast and of Drake Passage (a total of 25°)

27.8° S
21.3° W

Omission of coastline (B): Cape Frio to Bahia Blanca = loss of 16° of latitude and 20° of longitude. going southward

Omission (C). Drake Passage: = Loss of 9° more of latitude going southward

43.1° S
2.2° E

1. Annobon Islands
2. Cavally River
3. Cape Palmas
4. St. Paul River
5. Mano River
6. Freetown
7. Bijagos Islands
8. Gambia River
9. Dakar
10. Senegal River
11. Cape Blanc
12. Cape Juby
13. Sebu River
14. Gibraltar
15. Guadalquivir River
16. Cape St. Vincent
17. Tagus River
18. Cape Finisterre
19. Gironde River
20. Brest

21. Cape Verde Islands
22. The Canary Islands
23. Madeira Islands
24. The Azores
25. Cuba
   (a) Gulf of Guacanayabo
   (b) Guantanamo Bay
   (c) Bahia de Nipe
   (d) Bahia de la Gloria
   (e) Camaguey Mountains
   (f) Sierra Maestra Mountains
26. Andros Island
27. San Salvador (Watling)
28. Isle of Pines
29. Jamaica
30. Hispaniola
   (Santo Domingo, Haiti)
31. Puerto Rico
32. Rio Moroni
33. Corantijn River

34. Essequibo River
35. Orinoco River
36. Gulf of Venezuela
37. Pt. Gallinas
38. Magdalena River
39. Gulf of Uraba
40. Honduras (Cape Gracias a Dios)
41. Yucatan
42. Cape Frio
43. Salvador
44. San Francisco River
45. Recife (Pernambuco)
46. Cape Sao Roque
47. Rio Parahyba
48. Bahia Sao Marcos
49. Serras de Gurupi, de Desordam, de Negro
50. The Amazon (No. 1) Para River
51. The Amazon (No. 2) Para River
52. The Amazon (No. 2) western mouth

53. Island of Marajo
54. Essequibo River
55. Mouths of the Orinoco
56. Peninsula of Paria
57. Martinique
58. Guadaloupe
59. Antigua
60. Leeward Islands
61. Virgin Islands
62. Gulf of Venezuela
63. Magdalena River
64. Atrato River
65. Honduras (Cape Gracias a Dios)
66. Yucatan
67. Bahia Blanca
68. Rio Colorado
69. Gulf of San Mathias
70. Rio Negro (Argentina)
71. Rio Chubua
72. Gulf of San Gorge

73. Bahia Grande
74. Cape San Diego (near the Horn)
75. Falkland Islands
76. The South Shetlands
77. South Georgia
78. The Palmer Peninsula
79. The Weddell Sea
80. Mt. Ropke, Queen Maud Land
81. The Regula Range
82. Muhlig-Hofmann Mountains
83. Penck Trough
84. Neumeyer Escarpment
85. Drygalski Mountains
86. Vorposten Peak
87. Boreas, Passat Nunataks
88. Tristan d'Acunha
89. Gough Island
77. South Georgia
95. Fernando da Naronha

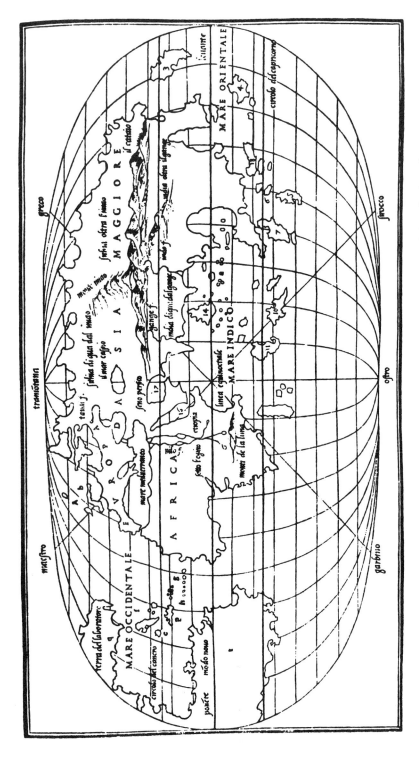

Benedetto Bordone Map of 1528 reflecting the vaguest notion of South America.

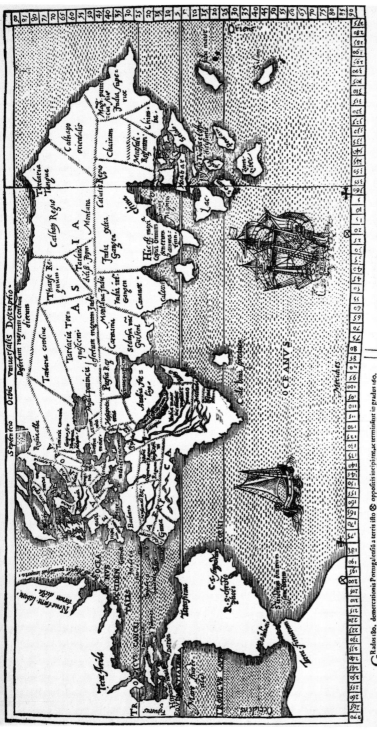

Robert Thorne Map of 1527 incorrectly placing the bulges of South America and Africa on the same longitude.

untenable *a priori*. It is supported not only by the testimony of Strabo concerning the maritime superiority of the preclassical thalassocrats over the classical Greeks and Romans down to Strabo's time (first centuries B.C. and A.D.), but also by the evidence of a science lost in classical antiquity though reflected in legends on record in classical and preclassical literature. For example, Hesiod (eighth century B.C.) tells us that the "iron" age in which he lived was preceded by an "age of heroes" far better than the men of his time.[39] The greatest sage of historic Egypt—creator of the architecture that produced the most monumental structures ever erected by man—was Imhotep, who flourished during the first half of the Early Bronze Age.

Mesopotamia cherished a tradition that at the dawn of civilization, long before any period of history known to us, science stood at a level from which historic man has fallen. Oannes brought from the sea knowledge and technology above anything achieved (or, for that matter, achievable) by Sumer, Babylonia, Assyria or classical Greek antiquity.[40]

The Hebrews have bequeathed to us the same story. We do not refer to the Paradise of indolent Adam and Eve in Eden (which can hardly be called a picture of scientific excellence), but rather to repeated echoes of an antiquity in which technology and wisdom were rooted. Genesis 4:17 in attributing the construction of cities to antediluvian times (legendarily expressed as the building of a city by Enoch son of Cain) ties in with the excavation of cities built in Neolithic times: certainly before 4000 B.C., and maybe as early as 7000 B.C. Genesis (5:28–29) goes on to tell us that in the days of Noah's father, Lemech, society was already stratified into its historic guild structure. Man had already developed the arts of agriculture (Genesis 4:12), and herding was established by tent-dwelling tribes who followed the grass supply for extensive grazing. The latter were viewed as a guild of specialists descended from an idealized ancestor (Jabal, Genesis 4:20). "Common law" from a remote antiquity was entrenched with blood revenge as the cornerstone of honor and justice (Genesis 4:8–15). The Universe was viewed as having an inbuilt morality pervaded as it was by the principle of Nemesis, for no crime could escape the attention of the just Ruler of the Universe (Genesis 4:10). People who transgressed the unwritten "common law" might evade the penalties of society—including the death penalty—but only at the price of a fate worse than death: homelessness and wandering without the protection of kith and kin (4:13–16). The struggle between farmer and herdsman was built into society from the start (Genesis 4:2ff.), but all concerned accepted the fact that they fit into one order, for the ancestors of the agriculturist and the herdsman were viewed as brothers: Cain and Abel (Genesis 4:2).

Urban culture implies technology beyond the arts of animal husbandry and farming. Lemech's son by Ada was Jubal, the "ancestor" (i.e., the prototype) of the guild of all musicians, whether they played stringed or wind instruments (Genesis 4:2). Lemech's son Tubal-Cain by his other wife Zillah was the "ancestor" of metallurgists both of copper or iron (Genesis 4:22). Noah is not simply a flood hero; he is depicted as a shipwright whose divinely inspired product could weather any storm (Genesis 6:13–8:14). His art included not only the use of choice timber but also of caulking (Genesis 6:14). Moreover, the use of birds which could be released for determining the presence and direction of land (Genesis 8:6–12) is not a folkloristic invention, but reflects actual navigational practice. Obviously, if the ancients sailed the seven seas before the age of literacy, they must have had a science and technology that gave them their capabilities. And if they lacked modern methods of science and instrumentation, they had other methods that enabled them to score their successes. A cage full of homing pigeons is not a bad method of direction finding. If it sounds quaint, it is only because we have devised methods more to our liking, but not necessarily better in all circumstances even today.

The sages known to later Israel harked back to the Heroic Age. Heman, Calcol and Darda were regarded as sons of Zerah and grandchildren of the eponymous ancestor of the tribe of Judah (1 Chronicles 2:6); Solomon's wisdom could only be measured against that of those sages of a distant past (1 Kings 3:12). Job, who was the greatest figure of antiquity according to Job 1:3, is classed with Noah and Daniel as heroic figures from a hoary past in Ezekiel 14:14, 20; that Daniel is singled out as the paragon of wisdom in Ezekiel 28:3.

Wisdom (*Hokma,* in Hebrew) includes science and technology: in Proverbs 24:3 it designates the architecture whereby a house is constructed. In Proverbs 3:19 God is represented as establishing the earth through wisdom, i.e., not merely by fiat as in Genesis, but by technology regarded as antedating history.

The American traditions are in the last analysis the same. What Oannes is to Mesopotamia, Quetzalcoatl (or Kukulcan) is to Mesoamerica. In the hoary past, the arts of civilization were introduced by an agent remembered with gratitude and admiration, though we can never hope to regain his blessings until the restoration of that Golden Age, to be ushered in when he returns as its messianic figure.[41]

The question arises: are all of these legends the inevitable and universal products of the human mind from one end of the earth to the other, wherever men may be? I doubt it, nor do we have to go farther than ourselves to find the exact opposite. Western man is geared to the proposition that what is ancient is primitive and what is truly scientific must be modern. Moreover, we have faith in evolution, which, prior to the current fears of worldwide nuclear destruction, implies that man and the world and certainly science are by the nature of things getting better and better. Modern man has been tacitly assuming that, having risen from the depths of barbarism, we are moving onward and upward to a paradise on earth through technological achievement, as though wisdom were born with us. I am inclined to see in the bygone Golden Ages of legends in the Old and New Worlds, the modified memories of a brilliant international past whose scattered traces provide us with sufficient clues for restoring it to the outline of history, and whose existence was rightly surmised by critical authors such as Strabo.

Before leaving the implications of the Piri Reis material, I cannot pass over in silence the implications of the map as first suspected by a little-known pioneer, the late Captain Arlington H. Mallery. Mallery observed that the Piri Reis map of 1513 indicates, more or less accurately, the shoreline of Antarctica that has been for millennia covered by an ice cap. I must refer the reader to Hapgood's ground-breaking *Maps of the Ancient Sea Kings* which has the startling subtitle *Evidence of Advanced Civilization in the Ice Age*. The chronological implications of Mallery and Hapgood rest on oceanographic factors that lie beyond my competence. What I am prepared to accept is that ancient mariners with the capability of transoceanic navigation flourished in preliterate times—certainly throughout the Bronze Age, and probably earlier. They made charts reflecting arts that were later forgotten: notably the determination of longitude. If I am not prepared to endorse Mallery's and Hapgood's retrojection of that civilization into Ice Age antiquity, it is because I do not master enough of the essential elements of information to express an independent judgment. But I am not inclined to brush their views aside as science fiction.

If I have learned anything throughout nearly half a century of study, it is to keep an open mind and to avoid confusing majority opinion with truth. Many seemingly preposterous myths have turned out to be correct. While savants "with both feet on the ground" were agreed that Troy was a fiction of Homer's poetic fancy, Schliemann, with the childish faith of an amateur, unearthed it. Notable breakthroughs often require the kind of thinking that "sound" people (i.e., who have the weight of consensus behind them) will brand as "unscientific" or plain "crazy." And to be quite frank, it is not always easy to determine the fine line that separates creative genius from unproductive nonsense. The only criteria we have are the results. "By their fruits shall ye know them." And here the element of luck enters the picture. Unconventional thinking, when it is crowned with success, is meritorious. But if it meets with failure, it reaps a harvest of ridicule and disgrace. Pioneers must be willing to take the chance.[42]

The solid citizen of academia would not think of expressing a great thought, even if one should perchance cross his mind, for "sensible" men who have achieved position and the emoluments of their professions are not tempted to jeopardize their reputations and security as crusaders in the cause of truth. Nor has anyone the right to ask the other fellow to run the risk of martyrdom in a world which is already tough enough.

In the Middle (2000–1600 B.C.) and Late Bronze Age (1600–1200 B.C.) a series of hardy megalithic structures were erected across the Mediterranean and into the Atlantic.[43] We do not imply that any structure fashioned of huge stones (megaliths) must have been erected by the same people who made other large stone buildings, regardless of time and place. Nor are we ruling out connections (albeit attenuated) with megalithic cultures in the Pacific—as far afield and as late as Easter Island. We are simply ignoring, for the time being, such problems because at this stage we will invest our efforts to more avail by reckoning only with the least attenuated and the best attested evidence.

In the last chapter we showed that, from at least the Middle Bronze Age, Egypt provided marine facilities (without the need for land connections) joining the Mediterranean-Atlantic waters with the Red Sea–Indian Ocean waters. We also observed that the chief motive for marine missions was not so much trade as such but the securing of the minerals needed by the international technologies without which no country or group of people could be in step with the times. There were primitive people in the interiors of Africa, Asia and Europe, but they were not in step with the civilized world. As a matter of fact, it was not until fairly late in the nineteenth century A.D. that large parts of the interior of Africa were even explored. The same can be said of about half of South America here and now.

We are dealing with a chain of megalithic structures on numerous islands and shores of the Mediterranean and Northeast Atlantic including Malta,[44] Sardinia, Minorca,[45] Majorca, Spain, Portugal, Brittany, Denmark, England and Ireland.[46] The links are unmistakable. For instance, a distinctively Mycenaean dagger was carved in antiquity on a megalith at Stonehenge, attesting connections between Britain and the Aegean ca. 1500 B.C.: [47] how directly or indirectly is another matter. Whether the same ships plied between one end and the other end of the network, or whether (and to what extent) they sailed from one port to the other, transferring the cargo at various staging areas or changing the crews (or at least the pilots specializing in the particular waters connecting only two of the points along the extensive sea-lane) need not be settled now.

The genetic relationship between megalithic structures from Malta to Stonehenge is borne out by interlocking major features and details. Their structure and orientation has to do with celestial phenomena. When scholars call Stonehenge an ancient observatory, astronomical computer, or scientific installation as well as a place of worship they are essentially right, however much we may question the precision of their terminology and detailed explanation of the function(s) of the structure. Malta and Stonehenge have unmistakable features in common including horseshoe formations. Moreover the spiral figures incised on these monuments tie in with the astronomical functions of the temples. It is the spiral form of the zodiac as clearly preserved in the examples from Egypt, notably from Dendera and Esna of the Roman period.[48] That we are not making an excessive leap in time and place is evident from the Phaistos Disc from Crete around the middle of the second millennium B.C.[49] The two spirals, one on each side of the Disc, are to be compared with a double spiral carved along the Holy of Holies of the Second Tarxien Temple on Malta.[50] That the Phaistos Disc is zodiacal is indicated by the identity of several pictographs: the lion for Leo, the bow for Sagittarius, the fish for Pisces, the scales for Libra, etc. The most telling link of the Phaistos Disc with the Egyptian zodiacs is Thueris, the Egyptian goddess with the crocodile's head.[51] She is on the Round Zodiac of Dendera, and appears four times on the Phaistos Disc. The analogues of the Disc in this and some other regards are with Egypt.

From island to island—and within each island—there are individual differences between the megalithic structures. Those in England differ from those on Malta, but those in England (or on Malta) differ markedly from each other. This is true of any dynamic tradition. Only an uninformed and uninterested person will say, "If you've seen one you've seen them all," of the pyramids of Egypt, of Greek temples, or of the megalithic Bronze Age temples. Egypt has step pyramids, bent pyramids, truncated pyramids and straight-sided pyramids coming to a point. Some pyramids have four sides; others, three. We need not waste our time or the reader's proving that no two Greek temples are alike—nor any two Egyptian or two American pyramids. Variation of megalithic structures in any specific area is lively and obvious to any observer. Minorca is full of megalithic structures of several categories. On that island, it happens that the spiral never appears as an ornamental design, but a keen observer has noted that some of the talayots are made not of horizontal stone courses laid one upon the other, but of one gently sloping spiral course winding upward to a narrow coil at the top. In other words, the spiral is expressed architecturally, as a cruciform church embodies the symbol of Christianity.

That the zodiac of the megalithic mariners does not reflect mere superstition (i.e., astrology) but goes hand in hand with astronomical science is indicated by the sophistication of installations like Stonehenge. The mariners needed a combination of the exact sciences on

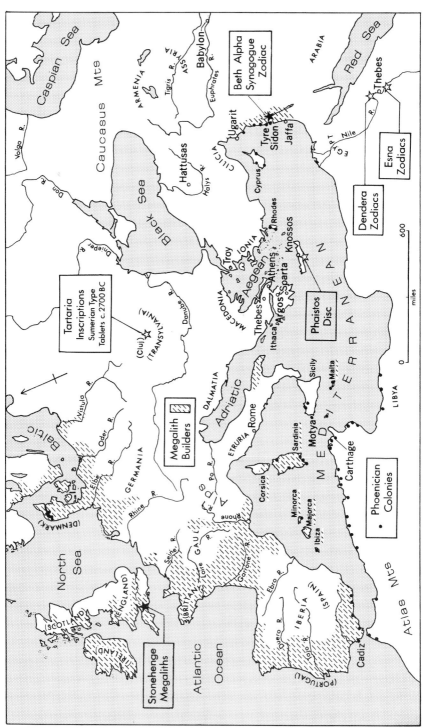

EUROPE AND MEDITERRANEAN

Caspian Sea

Red Sea

ARABIA

ARMENIA

ASSYRIA

Babylon

Tigris R.

Euphrates R.

Beth Alpha Synagogue Zodiac

Thebes

EGYPT

Nile R.

Esna Zodiacs

Caucasus Mts

Hattusas

CILICIA

Ugarit

Tyre
Sidon

Jaffa

Dendera Zodiacs

Black Sea

Volga R.

Don R.

Dnieper R.

Cyprus

Halys R.

Rhodes

Knossos

Danube R.

Troy

IONIA

Aegean

Athens

Argos

Sparta

Phaistos Disc

600

miles

Tartaria Inscriptions Sumerian Type Tablets c. 2700 BC

(Cluj)
(TRANSYLVANIA)

MACEDONIA

Thebes

Ithaca

0

MEDITERRANEAN

Megalith Builders

DALMATIA

Adriatic

ALPS

Rome

ETRURIA

Po R.

Sicily

Malta

LIBYA

Baltic

Vistula R.

Oder R.

Elbe R.

GERMANIA

Rhine R.

Sardinia

Corsica

Motya

Carthage

Phoenician Colonies

(DENMARK)

North Sea

GAUL

Seine R.

Loire R.

Rhone R.

Garonne R.

Minorca

Majorca

Ibiza

(SCOTLAND)

(ENGLAND)

(IRELAND)

(BRITAIN)

Atlantic Ocean

Ebro R.

IBERIA

(SPAIN)

Duero R.

Tajo R.

(PORTUGAL)

Cadiz

Atlas Mts

Stonehenge Megaliths

which their celestial navigation was founded. To go to far-off shores in quest of minerals meant that they had to reach specific destinations and get back again with precision. Their way of life precluded aimless wandering. Thus in the Bronze Age, the tin of England was needed for hardening copper into bronze. The merchant marine way of life was based on technologies, instrumentations and sciences: not on religion and magic alone.

So deep-seated was the ancients' concern for celestial knowledge that it has shaped all of subsequent human history down to our own day. Man has reached the Moon and is preparing to visit the planets, in fulfilment of a vision that began with the requirements of ancient life, evoking the science of astronomy based on observation in the Stone Age. On seas (and desert wastes), where there are no landmarks, the path of man was not on earth but in heaven. This is the plain meaning of celestial navigation. Preoccupation with the details of the heavenly bodies and their movements was so important that it took on a religious dimension. The Sun, the Moon, and each star were not only bodies in space, but were invested with personalities. The planet we call Venus was personified as the Babylonian goddess Ishtar.[52] The Greeks, in taking over the astronomy of the older civilization (for the latter had spread widely in pre-Greek times into what was to become the Greek World), also translated the name of the planet to the corresponding Greek goddess's name: Aphrodite. The Romans did the same thing: translating Aphrodite from Greek to Latin (i.e., Venus). We have accepted the Roman terminology for modern astronomy without bothering to Anglicize "Venus."

Astral religion has always confronted the monotheisms with a sticky problem. It is one thing to tell the believer that it is unqualifiedly wrong to worship images of fertility gods like Baal and Anath, for they are merely wood or stone fashioned by the hands of man into images that God's people have no business worshiping. But what is to be done about adoring the Sun, Moon and starry heavens? Are they not the creations of God, as stated in Scripture?

A case can always be made, without any tinge of sacrilege, that in a reverent appreciation of the heavenly bodies, we are also rendering homage to God, the creator of the Universe. Starting with Genesis 1, the Bible extols the creation of the Sun, Moon and stars which are indispensable parts of the universe established by God. As the Psalmist (8:3) says: "For I see Thy heavens, the work of Thy fingers: the moon and stars which Thou hast created." For the Hebrew poet, austere monotheism could not be allowed (for literary, if for no other reasons) to eliminate the climate of aesthetic expression. Accordingly, the Psalmist and the author of Job felt no need to isolate God in awful monotheistic loneliness, but borrowed from the older mythology the heavenly host that peoples His divine court. Thus Job 2:1 narrates that "Once upon a time, the sons of god [i.e., the pantheon] took their stations next to Yahweh and also among them Satan took his station by Yahweh."

The need of the Hebrew dramatist to draw on the already ancient mythology is no more polytheistic than the puritanic Christian Milton's incorporation of so much classical mythology in *Paradise Lost*. In Job 38:7 the poet tells us that Yahweh created the universe "when the stars of morning sang together, and all the sons of god shouted." Here the stars are the deities who populate God's heavenly court. No matter how pure Judeo-Christian monotheism tries to become, it is well-nigh impossible to divest it of our astral heritage whose roots are in the Stone Age.

The rabbis expressed the dilemma quite well. The Talmud includes a tractate on paganism. The Hebrew term for paganism is *Avodah Zarah* "Alien Worship": and idolatry is often called *ᶜakum* (*ᶜa* stands for *ᶜavodat* "worship [of]"; *k* for *kokavim* "stars"; *u* means "and"; *m* stands for *mazzalot* "constellations"). Thus *ᶜakum* "idolatry" literally means "the worship of stars and constellations." The question arises: if we are not to worship the heavenly bodies, why did God create them, placing in our way a temptation that can undo us? Obviously the rabbis did not sanction idolatry in any form including "the worship of stars and constellations," and yet they had the sense to analyze the problem rationally. The sun, moon and stars were created by God as an indispensable part of the universal order. Must God destroy the Universe (asked the rabbis rhetorically) just because fools would pervert the natural purpose of the heavenly bodies into objects of idolatry? [53]

Astronomy not only fed astral religion, but also the astral superstition that we call astrology, which retains its popularity unabated to this day in an age that we like to call truly scientific.

What emerges is the fact that our science, religion and magic are interrelated and intertwined. The magical use of the signs of the zodiac cannot be divorced from religion, on the one hand, nor from the exact science of astronomy on the other. Moreover, there is no evidence for the supposed progression from magic, to religion, to science in our culture.[54] To the contrary, we have every reason to detect science from the very start of anything that we can meaningfully call human development. Neolithic (and perhaps still earlier) man developed, for practical reasons, the science of astronomy and its concomitant mathematical and physical sciences. There is no reason to believe that superstition and magic came first, true religion came next, and at last we enter the crowning stage of science. Superstitions concerning lucky (e.g., 7) and unlucky (e.g., 13) numbers [55] presume arithmetical if not mathematical systems; just as lucky and unlucky stars must be preceded by some astronomical system.

The subject has many implications. Gods can be earth deities, or can reside in stones or trees. If we can speculate on the mentality of primitive "men" before the dawn of astronomy, it might seem that he was more concerned with the earth around him than with heaven so far above him. Yet *our* traditional religious imagery of *our* "Heavenly Father" who dwells in the sky developed in the wake of astronomy.

Failure to reckon with such matters leads us into pitfalls when interpreting history. For instance, it has been generally (though more or less tacitly) assumed that the mosaic zodiacs in synagogues of the Roman and Byzantine periods were merely decorative.[56] *A priori* this never made sense, for it implied that one of the most prominent and frequent features of the synagogue had absolutely nothing to do with the religion for which the buildings were constructed. The very fact that the zodiacs came as such a surprise to us should have evoked a more searching inquiry. In the Old Testament, several different kinds of paganism are condemned as we have already noted. There was no doubt about the verdict against fertility gods such as Baal and Anath. Given the premises of Yahwism, no place was left for worshiping such Canaanite deities, and though it took a long time to stamp out their cults, the outcome was a foregone conclusion. The Old Testament also inveighs against astral religion, for Yahwistic Hebrews were worshiping and bowing down to the Sun, Moon and the whole host of heaven. We have already explained why astral religion had a function and a place within Biblical monotheism. For a Hebrew to deny the existence of, and scorn, Baal and Anath was natural and right; whereas, to scorn the heavenly host was to blaspheme God's creation and to deny the order of things, which is not only sacrilege but irrational. For this reason, astral religion and astrology found a place in brands of Judaism such as the one that produced the synagogues with mosaic zodiacs in Roman and Byzantine times. This is confirmed by the discovery of a sectarian Jewish scroll, of the Roman period, incorporating astrology and the zodiac.[57]

That the Jews did not borrow astrology outright from their Greco-Roman neighbors is clear from the fact that the Hebrew names for the signs of the zodiac in these mosaics are not always translations from the Greek. For example, instead of Aquarius, we find d^eli "bucket." Therefore there was a native Hebrew tradition of the zodiac. The finest of the synagogue mosaics is at Beth Alpha in Israel, where the twelve signs of the zodiac surround the central figure of Helios driving his chariot drawn by four steeds. It is quite probable that the Jewish sectarians who worshiped in the Beth Alpha synagogue identified Helios with Yahweh, who is described in Psalm 19:1-7 presiding over the universe as the sun (N.B. v. 6) with the heavenly bodies attesting His majesty: "The heavens tell God's glory, yea the firmament declares the deeds of His hands. (3) Day utters speech to day, and night imparts knowledge to night. (4) There is no speech and there are no words whose sound is not heard. (5) Their voice goes forth throughout all the earth; in the ends of the world are their words; for the Sun He has placed a tent therein. (6) For He rises (in the east) as a bridegroom from his canopy, rejoicing as a hero running a course. (7) At the end of the heavens is His setting place (in the west) and His rounds are by their extremity, nor is aught hidden from His wrath." Since the Psalmist likens God to the Sun, exalted by the heavenly bodies, the Jewish sectarians had the best possible authority for portraying God as the Sun, surrounded by the constellations that attest His glory.

Normative Judaism and Christianity have succeeded in eliminating astrology from official religion, but only through conscious and sustained efforts.

The achievements of civilized man in preliterate times, prior to the building of the first cities in Neolithic antiquity, include a high development of the exact sciences and technologies. Cuneiform literature,[58] notably the Gilgamesh Epic, reflects what the archeology of Neolithic Mesopotamia illustrates: (1) access to raw materials in many far-off areas, (2) development of land and sea travel, (3) domestic, urban and naval architecture, (4) skilled workmanship in ceramics, stone-cutting and metallurgy, (5) the stratification of society into specialized guilds, (6) city planning, (7) an already ancient tradition of science and technology, (8) a system of international morality and law in addition to local regulations of law and order—in brief, an international ecumene. The distribution of the same general system of science and technology is reflected by the same salient features of high culture over the face of the globe in both the Old and New Worlds. The reason we have singled out the megalithic temples, tombs and astronomical observatories of the Bronze Age mariners is that their monuments are still standing in Mediterranean and Atlantic areas attesting their science, technologies, religion and navigational accomplishments, and outlining the nature and extent of their vast network. Such achievements cannot be the gropings of primitive men, but are rather the culmination of a long development from a remote past.

If we compare the march of science from A.D. 1800 to 1970, there is no doubt that the period is marked by technological progress. But if we compare the science of the Golden Ages of antiquity with that of the Middle Ages, it is more difficult to maintain the doctrine of "the later, the better." The level reflected in the Egyptian medicine that produced the Edwin Smith Surgical Papyrus [59] is higher than the level of medicine in America during the days of the American Revolution.[60] George Washington was literally bled to death by the medical establishment of his day. Imhotep was a more accomplished architect than any Colonial American. There were ancient mariners in a remote, preliterate past who could determine longitude, which modern science could not duplicate until the eighteenth century A.D. Worldwide exploration and interconnections were more highly developed in the Bronze Age than in Europe before the Age of Columbus and Magellan.

The megalithic monuments of the Bronze Age mariners are tangible reminders of a world civilization, with highly developed science and technologies, long before we can speak of Greeks or Hebrews. In certain ways, such as in navigation and geography, the Greco-Roman world was inferior to that Golden Age of old, as Strabo rightly infers.

Chapter V

THE METCALF STONE
AND ANCIENT WRITING

I N 1 9 6 6 Manfred Metcalf made a discovery in the ruins of Underwood Mill, on land belonging to Fort Benning, Georgia. The Mill was built in the nineteenth century, well before Sir Arthur Evans excavated the first Minoan inscriptions at Knossos in 1900. Metcalf was looking for slabs to be used in building a barbecue pit. On cleaning one of them that he had pried loose from the moldering Mill walls, he saw it was inscribed. Good judgment prompted him to transmit the Stone to Dr. Joseph B. Mahan, Jr., Director of Education and Research, at the nearby Columbus Museum of Arts and Crafts, Columbus, Georgia.

Mahan, an expert on American Indian ethnology and archeology, has been specializing on the Yuchis, who once inhabited the area, but who were forced out and, in 1836, were resettled in Oklahoma where they still perpetuate their ancestral religion. He had noted that one of the Yuchi agricultural festivals had too many general and detailed resemblances to the Feast of Tabernacles prescribed in Leviticus 23 to be accidental. He suspected that both the Hebrew and Yuchi celebrations were reflexes of the same East Mediterranean milieu of the Bronze Age.

As in Leviticus 23, the Yuchis celebrate (1) an eight-day festival, (2) that starts on the fifteenth day (or full moon) of the holy harvest month; throughout the holiday, they (3) live in "booths," (4) at the cultic center, where (5) they nurture a sacred fire. To this day the

Jews also observe the first three of these features. They have given up the fourth, because after the destruction of their temples in Jerusalem and their dispersal throughout the world, they had no cultic center to which the pilgrimages could be made. The Jews have also discontinued the fifth point, the fire, because it is associated with the sacrifices, all of which have been suspended since the loss of the Second Temple in A.D. 70.

Like the Yuchis, observant Jews start their holiday on the full moon [61] and dwell in booths. The latter are constructed with open spaces in the roof which are covered during the festival with branches, foliage, fruits and vegetables, much like the Yuchi booths with open spaces in the roof covered with branches and foliage for the holiday.

Both the Jews and the Yuchis form processions making circumambulations on the festival. The Jews do this in the synagogue; the Yuchis, around the fire in the sacred cultic area. In the Yuchi processions, a couple of men carry each a large, foliage-crested branch, as they accompany the community in their circumambulations. At other times during the celebration, larger numbers of men shake such foliage-crested branches. The Jews have a similar custom; on Tabernacles they shake the *lûlāv:* a prescribed combination of plants lashed together into a ceremonial staff specially for this festival.

Neither Mahan nor I believe that the Yuchis are "one of the Ten Lost Tribes," nor is there any evidence showing that they stem from any segment of the Jewish people. It is, rather, our view that both the Yuchis and the ancient Hebrews share certain cultural features rooted in the same ancient East Mediterranean of the Bronze Age. Accordingly, Mahan suspected that the Metcalf Stone, found on old Yuchi terrain, might be inscribed in a system of writing with Near East origins in the second millennium B.C. In May 1968, Mahan sent me a cast of the Stone with a request for my opinion.

The affinities of the script are with the Aegean of the latter half of the second millennium B.C. In form the signs go with those of the Aegean syllabary, represented by Minoan Linear A and Mycenaean Linear B. Two of the signs on the Metcalf Stone might be compared (as we shall note below) with syllabic symbols in Linear A and B, or alternatively with letters of the Phoenician alphabet. Should the latter turn out to be correct, the Stone might be said to reflect a stage intermediate between the syllabary and alphabet.[62]

The Metcalf Stone.

The double axe in the lower left corner is familiar in Minoan culture, but it also occurs widely in antiquity out into the Atlantic World,
from Stonehenge to America. The single vertical lines remind us of the
vertical line that stands for the numeral "1" in the Aegean syllabary;
and the little circles might each stand for "100" as in that syllabary.
The spoked circle at the beginning of the third line might be a pictograph of the sun, but I think it is more likely a large number like
"1,000" or "10,000." In Minoan a circle with four spokes equals
"1,000." On the Metcalf Stone there are seven spokes suggesting that
if "1,000" is not the value, perhaps it is some larger number like
"10,000" (though "700" or "7,000" also come to mind as possibilities). That we are dealing with numerals is supported by the last sign
(i.e., on the far right) of the first line. It is the syllable *da* in Linear A
and B, used idiomatically after numbers in Linear B inventories. There
is also a sign closely resembling a Linear B fraction. At the beginning
of line 2 is the *rá* sign of Linear A and B.

Two signs can be compared in shape with Aegean syllabic symbols
or with letters of the Phoenician alphabet. The opening sign in line one
may be compared with either the *tá* sign of Linear A and B, or with
the letter *d* (Phoenician *dalet* = Greek *delta*). Similarly the final sign
on line 3, may be compared with the *su* sign of Linear A and B, on the
one hand, or with alphabetic *b* (*beth* in Phoenician = Greek *beta*).
The final sign of the Stone resembles the oxhide ingot of Linear A
and B, suggesting that the text might be an inventory of commodities.
But it is premature to try to interpret the Stone. At this stage we must
content ourselves with placing, as best we can, the system of writing
in historic perspective.

If the Metcalf Stone were the only example of New World writing
that suggested Mediterranean affinities, there would be little value in
pursuing the matter further. However, other inscriptions in Mesoamerica independently point in the same direction. Pierre Honoré
has suggested resemblances between Mayan and Cretan writing.[63] Although general graphic similarities may be accidental, some of them
are too detailed to be brushed aside.[64]

The evidence for historic relationship has grown with the observation by Svein-Magnus Grodys of Oslo, Norway, that a number of Aztec glyphs cannot be divorced from strikingly similar signs on the

Phaistos Disc from Crete of the mid-second millennium B.C. For example, the head with the feathered headdress is not merely a similarity in design, but it also reflects a cultural trait linking American Indians with the Sea People (such as the Minoans and Philistines) of the Mediterranean in the second millennium B.C. The object resembling a studded club has not been identified, but it is so distinctive and detailed that there is no denying that the same object is depicted in Crete and Mexico. The same may be said for the "dotted circle."

Unlike Mayan writing, the Aztec glyphs do not seem to have been used for recording regular texts. Grodys' explanation is of more than passing interest for it suggests a new avenue of historic investigation. He believes that when warlords moved on to conquer and settle in new lands, they carried their "coats of arms" with them. He maintains that the Aztec glyphs were carried by Old World warriors, as the heraldic emblems of their noble families, to the ends of the earth wherever they invaded and imposed their rule on the defeated natives.

There is more to Grodys' view than meets the eye. Heraldic emblems appear on seal cylinders of Mesopotamia,[65] to identify people of consequence, as early as the fourth millennium B.C., and there is nothing preposterous about such "coats of arms" being carried by warlords to distant lands in antiquity.

Actually the relations between Old and New World writing go still deeper, involving the origin of the very alphabet that we still use. Our alphabet is generally regarded as originating with the Phoenicians, then transmitted to the Greeks, and by the latter to the Romans. A number of theories have been propounded to show that the Phoenicians got the idea from one or another known people such as the Egyptians, Babylonians or Minoans.[66] That there was some interplay among these and other literate peoples is likely, because they, with their methods of writing, intermingled during the second millennium in the East Mediterranean. Thus at Ugarit, texts of the Late Bronze Age have been found in Babylonian cuneiform, Egyptian hieroglyphs, the Aegean syllabary, hieroglyphic Hittite and of course the native Ugaritic alphabet. The latter was patterned after the Phoenician ABC not only as to certain letter forms but even in the same sequence of letters familiar to us in the Hebrew, Greek and Latin forms of the alphabet. But there is another element to be considered:

The maritime factor in history was of major importance in a number of critical periods during remote antiquity—starting well before the Early Bronze Age. The early Sumerian cities for example appeared in the fourth millennium (in Chalcolithic times) in southern Babylonia, within easy reach of the Persian Gulf. Moreover, the native tradition had it that civilization was brought by beings via those waters. The same holds for Mesoamerica, where the pre-Columbian population cherished a consistent tradition that civilization had been brought by Quetzalcoatl (variant, Kukulcan) by ship. Sailing on the open seas required the development of celestial navigation. Moreover, keeping track of time was important for many reasons. Sailing instructions require not only direction-finding, but also time reckoning. A captain must know how many days are needed for reaching a destination. Calendrical methods were necessary, not only for reckoning with the solar year and its seasons, but for keeping track of the days in the lunar month. Distances from port to port, even on ancient ocean voyages, normally require not years so much as months and days. Accordingly they composed lunar as well as solar zodiacs. Another requirement for the mariners was the keeping of records both for inscribing the log, and for the bookkeeping essential in commerce. Practical men like the ancient mariners needed a sensible and simple method of filling their needs. The cumbersome scripts of Egypt, Mesopotamia and China were all right for established, land-based cultures capable of maintaining an elaborate school system with many years of instruction before a scribe could qualify for his profession. Sea People needed some literate personnel for every operational unit—which happens to be the individual ship. Since the vessels were by modern standards quite small, a system of writing that could be learned quickly was required. The alphabet—usually ranging between twenty and thirty letters—made sense, and it is no accident that a Sea People, the Phoenicians, employed the alphabet and transmitted it to Europe.

The remarkable thing about the alphabet is that it was not limited to its familiar function of spelling words phonetically; it also served as a numerical system and as a method of keeping track of the days in a month.

In an important book entitled *The Alphabet and the Ancient Calendar Signs* (1953), Hugh A. Moran developed the thesis that the letters of the phonetic alphabet are based on the signs of an Old World lunar zodiac. It remained for David H. Kelley to bring the New World evidence into the picture. Under their joint authorship the book has appeared in a revised and expanded second edition (Daily Press, 856 San Antonio Road, Palo Alto, California, 1969). The contents of that volume, plus a number of private communications from Kelley, evoke new avenues of investigation that we shall examine, after discussing some related phenomena that fit into the picture at this juncture.

We have already mentioned the Phaistos Disc from Minoan Crete. It is made of clay impressed while still wet with dies for each pictograph. In other words, it is an early form of printing. The text is written spirally. Light on the Phaistos Disc comes from Roman Egypt, for the Round Zodiac of Dendera has striking similarities to the Disc. Both texts are inscribed spirally and contain astral symbols. The Dendera Zodiac includes Leo, Taurus, Capricorn, Cancer, Pisces, in their recognizable animal forms; Libra is represented by the usual scales; Sagittarius is suggested by two different archers: one a goddess, another a Pegasus (actually a human-torsoed, winged quadruped); but most important for our investigation is a large figure of Thueris (a hippopotamus-headed woman with human arms but animal legs) in the center. Thueris enjoyed wide appeal, and she appears four times on the Phaistos Disc. The Disc also has pictograms of the scales, fish, horn, bow, and lion head, suggesting respectively Libra, Pisces, Taurus, Sagittarius and Leo. There are still other signs that seem to appear on both documents: a large circle (containing five objects on the Phaistos Disc but eight on the Dendera Zodiac); the Dendera decapitated beast may be compared with the headless animal hide on the Phaistos Disc; a number of boats at Dendera recall the repeated boat sign of the Phaistos Disc; the Dendera ox leg (including thigh) calls to mind the Phaistos ox leg (albeit sans thigh). The spiral format and the duplication of so many distinctive signs (notably Thueris) link the two texts organically despite the time gap that separates them. Though they come from different parts of the East Mediterranean and are separated by a millennium and a half, they are as close as they are because of the conservative nature of astrology. A number of the signs on the Disc have phonetic values both there and (with simplifications in form) in Linear A and B.[67] In other words, some of the phonetic

Side A, Phaistos Disc. COURTESY, HARRY N. ABRAMS, INC., FROM *Crete and Mycenae*

Side B, Phaistos Disc. COURTESY, HARRY N. ABRAMS, INC.
FROM *Crete and Mycenae*

symbols in Aegean writing are now traced to specific zodiacal signs.
Hugh Moran and David Kelley have rendered a conspicuous service
in pointing to the interplay between the ancient calendar signs and the
alphabet. The calendar signs are largely lists to designate the days of
the "month," but the length of the "months" varies in different traditions. The most realistic lunar alphabet happens to be the oldest known
form of our alphabet arranged by the ancient scribes in a fixed sequence: to wit, the Ugaritic alphabet of the Late Bronze Age. The
Ugaritic alphabet, which we shall discuss below, has 29 letters, with
a phonetically superfluous 30th letter, corresponding exactly to the
length of the lunar month which vacillates between 29 and 30 days.
But lists of signs for days in the month vary greatly; a Malayan list
has 30, while a Chinese list has 28, while certain Greek, Tamil and
Cambodian lists have 27 (Moran-Kelley, op. cit., p. 175). Middle
American lists of the Maya and Aztecs have only 20 signs corresponding to the number of days in their "month." But this can be explained:
the Maya year, like the Egyptian year, has 360 days plus five epagome-
nal days, bringing the total to 365: the whole number closest to the
actual solar year. In Egypt, the 360 days were divided into 12 months
of 30 days each. The Maya had, instead, 18 months of 20 days each.
Now it is interesting to note that the standard Greek alphabet of 24
letters has only twenty ancient letters that it inherited from the Semites;
the last four letters (phi, chi, psi and omega) are Greek innovations
and were added to the first 20 that retain the same order they occupy
in the Ugaritic alphabet. (The rationale of "20" may be the fact that
such is the number of our fingers and toes: man's natural "digital computer.") On the other hand there is reason to regard the last three
letters of the 30-letter Ugaritic alphabet as added to an original alphabet of 27 letters, corresponding to the length of day-name sequences
found among Greeks, Tamils and Cambodians. (The rationale of "27"
may be sought in the predilection for triads and enneads that we find
in the ancient Near East. In both Egypt and Greece we find a "week"
of nine days; [68] three such "weeks" total 27 days.) The Arabic alphabet of 28 letters confronts us with the same number as the Chinese list
of 28. (The rationale of "28" may be sought in the fact that four weeks
of seven days total 28. Four and seven are important numbers in antiquity, and both figure prominently in time reckoning.)
The wide distribution of *related* lunar lists in both hemispheres re-

flects an ancient global network of mariners sharing basic elements of a common culture. It can not be the legacy of primitive and isolated Stone Age men, for it goes hand in hand with astronomy, calendrics and writing.

If we scrutinize the "Phoenician" alphabet, whose letter names we know from Hebrew tradition, a relation to the zodiac signs, including the lunar lists, is evident. The first letter, *alef* (Greek *alpha*), designates "ox," which we are to compare not merely with the animal but "bull" sign of the zodiac called Taurus.[69] The second letter of the alphabet, *bet* (Greek *beta*), means "house," which should be compared with the Aztec day-name *calli* "house." The tenth and eleventh letters, *yod* and *kaf* (Greek *iota* and *kappa*), both mean "hand," which we compare with the seventh day-name in the Maya list: *manik* "hand." The 12th Phoenician letter is *lamed* (Greek *lambda*) which cannot be dissociated from Maya *lamat* (variant *lambat*), which is the deified numeral "12." The 13th Phoenician letter, *mem* "water" (Greek *mu,* which is the form that the Egypto-Semitic word for "water" takes in Egyptian and Akkadian), is to be compared with the Maya day-name *muluk* "water" (*mu* in the Ixil dialect; cf. Quiche *mu* "wet"). The direct sequence of *k-l-m* (which we have inherited through the Greeks from the Phoenicians) thus corresponds to the direct Maya sequence of HAND, *lamat,* WATER, as noted by Kelley in confirmation of the hypothesis developed by Moran.

The 14th and 15th letters of the Phoenician alphabet are *nun* and *samekh,* respectively, both meaning "fish," with which we compare the zodiacal sign Pisces, familiarly represented as two fish. (It may be significant that if the 22-letter alphabet of the Phoenicians and Hebrews is reduced so that "hand" and "fish" are represented only once instead of twice each, we have a 20-letter sequence corresponding to the Mayan day-names and the 20-letter sequence presented by the Greek alphabet when stripped of its four, chronologically late, final letters.)

The 17th Phoenician letter, *pe* "mouth," belongs to the category of parts of the body, such as "hand" which we have discussed, and "head" and "tooth" which will be taken up below.

The 18th letter, *ṣade,* is defined by Moran as an "arrow and corresponding to the Chinese lunar mansion Chang (variant ts'ang) 'to shoot an arrow,' " which suggests Sagittarius.

The 19th letter, *qof,* means "monkey," synonymous with the 11th or "monkey" day in the Aztec and Maya lists of day-names. I am inclined to attach importance to the fact that "monkey" comes after the HAND, *lamat,* WATER sequence in the Phoenician alphabet as well as in the American day lists.

The 20th letter is *resh* "head" (Greek *ro*), while the 21st is *shin,* "tooth": both parts of the body. The Maya day-name *eb* can also mean "tooth."

The final Phoenician letter, the 22nd, is *taw* "cross," which we may compare with the constellation Crux ("Cross"). The fact that the Southern Cross is now seen only in the Southern Hemisphere is no counterindication. The ancient mariners were not confined to the waters north of the equator. Besides, if we go back far enough in antiquity the Cross was visible in the Northern Hemisphere.

The nature and history of our alphabet are more remarkable than meets the eye. Phonetically, the achievement is breathtaking for it is associated with a very fundamental and useful discovery: phonemic spelling. It happens that in the Semitic languages there are 29 distinctive consonantal sounds. By "distinctive" we mean that substituting any other distinctive sound in the language may change the meaning of the word. In English *p* and *b* are distinctive sounds (or, to use the terminology of linguistic science, are different phonemes in English), because "pull" and "bull" (or "pad" and "bad") have different meanings. The distinction, however, between *p* and *b* is not phonemic in Arabic. The word for "police" can be pronounced *polîs* or *bolîs;* and the word for "trousers" can be pronounced *pantalôn* or *bantalôn;* substituting *p* for *b,* or vice versa, never affects the meaning of an Arabic word. Most languages have between 20 and 35 phonemes, which means that the alphabetic principle (which implies "one and only one graphic sign for each phoneme in the language") enables us to spell any word with between 20 and 35 graphic signs depending on the phonemic pattern of the particular language.

The alphabet is the most useful single invention made by man throughout all his history. With the ancient cumbersome systems of writing like the Mesopotamian, Egyptian and Chinese, popular literacy is impossible. The alphabet with such a limited repertoire of signs brought literacy within the grasp of whole nations and made universal education possible.

The view of Moran and Kelley that zodiacal signs, arranged in lists to keep track of the days of the month, were also used to form systems of writing, including our own alphabet, is substantiated. There are zodiacal pictographs on the Phaistos Disc which were developed into phonetic signs of the Aegean syllabary. The Hebrew names of the alphabetic letters confirm their zodiacal origin, while the Ugaritic alphabet preserves the function of keeping track of the days of the lunar month by equaling the number of days from new moon to new moon. All of this points to a basic connection between the lunar zodiacs and the systems of writing that resulted in the alphabet.

The comparative study of the Old and New World zodiacs and writing systems will require rewriting the history of the alphabet. One of the striking results of this study concerns the origin of the phonemic principle ("one and only one symbol for each distinctive sound within the pattern of the specific language"). The acrophonic principle (whereby a symbol stands for the first sound in the name of the symbol) limited the sounds in the Hebrew-Phoenician alphabet to consonants, because in the ancient West Semitic languages all words begin with consonants. Thus *bet* stands for *b; gimil,* for *g; dalet,* for *d;* etc. There are no exceptions. Apparent exceptions, like *'alef,* are not real; for the *'alef* stands for consonantal *'* (not for the vowel *a* as it came to represent in our derived form of the alphabet among non-Semites). A consonantal *'alef* is the glottal catch which we subconsciously require between vowels with a diëresis; e.g., between the *o*'s in "coöperation." The number of consonantal phonemes in pure Semitic is 29, which is the closest possible whole number to the number of days in a lunar month (actually a little less than 29½ days). Thus the great discovery of the phonemic principle by the developers of the alphabet was subconscious. They were brought to it automatically by the fact that the consonantal phonemes in their language happens to approximate, as closely as is mathematically possible, the number of days in a lunar month.

The order of the letters of the alphabet goes back to remote antiquity. At Ugarit by 1400 B.C., it was fixed in the order which we can still detect in our modern ABC. To bring this out, we shall align with the Ugaritic ABC, the Hebrew-Phoenician, Greek and Latin forms of the alphabet insofar as they are transmitted in the same order:

	UGARITIC	PHOENICIAN-HEBREW	GREEK	LATIN
1.	a	a	a	a
2.	b	b	b	b
3.	g	g	g	c [70]
4.	ḫ			
5.	d	d	d	d
6.	h	h	e	e
7.	w	w	F	f
8.	z	z	z	
9.	ḥ	ḥ	h	h
10.	ṭ	ṭ	t[h] [71]	
11.	y	y	i	i/j [72]
12.	k	k	k	k
13.	š̆			
14.	l	l	l	l
15.	m	m	m	m
16.	ḏ			
17.	n	n	n	n
18.	ẓ			
19.	s	s	ks [73]	
20.	ʿ	ʿ	o [74]	o
21.	p	p	p	p
22.	ṣ	ṣ		
23.	q	q	q [75]	q
24.	r	r	r	r
25.	ṯ	sh	s [76]	s
26.	ǵ			
27.	t	t	t	t
28.	i			
29.	u		u	u
30.	ś			

The achievement of the ancients in inventing the phonemic alphabet would be noteworthy even had there been no complicating factors. The fact that the alphabet served as a lunar calendar as well as an amazingly simple system of writing makes matters more remarkable. But there was a third function of the alphabet: it served as a numeral system. The Hebrew letters have the following fixed numerical values:

Hebrew Letter	Numerical Value	Hebrew Letter	Numerical Value
a	1	l	30
b	2	m	40
g	3	n	50
d	4	s	60
h	5	c	70
w	6	p	80
z	7	ṣ	90
ḥ	8	q	100
ṭ	9	r	200
y	10	sh	300
k	20	t	400

So ingrained are the numerical values of the letters that when the Arabs took over the alphabetic principle and adjusted it to their own phonetic requirements, they rearranged the order of the letters drastically but retained the old numerical values of every letter that exists in the Hebrew alphabet. (See facing page.)

If the inventors of the alphabet had only reckoned with one problem, their product would have been one of the miracles of human ingenuity making possible popular literacy, in place of the elite literacy imposed by the cumbersome systems of Mesopotamia, Egypt or China. But instead, the alphabet has emerged from a device serving three dif-

Arabic Letter	Hebrew Letter	Numerical Value
a	a	1
b	b	2
t̲	t	400
t		500
j	g	3
ḥ	ḥ	8
h̬		600
d	d	4
d̲		700
r	r	200
z	z	7
s	s	60
sh	sh	300
ṣ	ṣ	90
ḍ		800
ṭ	ṭ	9
t̤		900
ꜥ	ꜥ	70
ǵ		1,000
f	p	80
q	q	100
k	k	20
l	l	30
m	m	40
n	n	50
h	h	5
w	w	6
y	y	10

ferent functions simultaneously: arithmetic, calendric and phonetic.

The alphabet can no longer be regarded as a sudden invention by an inspired individual or team of people in a specific area. It is rather the culmination of a long international development on the part of a network of merchant mariners whose activities spanned the Old World and the New. Behind the accomplishment lay millennia of civilization —some of it known, but most of it forgotten—shaped painstakingly by men on every sea and continent. Far from being primitive, those men were advanced in science and technology. They fostered mathematics, astronomy and time reckoning, as well as the techniques that made possible land and naval architecture, navigation and cartography. They spread the principles of economics, law and religion, as well as the arts of agriculture, animal husbandry, weaving, ceramics and metallurgy. It was they who developed writing: the factor that makes the study of history possible.

Chapter VI

SEA PEOPLE

W E H A V E R E V I E W E D enough evidence to show that Sea People in remote antiquity established and maintained sea-lanes so extensively that from the start all high civilizations formed one ecumene. The most startling document is the map of Piri Reis, which, as we stated earlier, implies not only the discovery of America in antiquity but also the ability of the ancient navigators to determine longitude. Most sensational of all is the mapping of the north coastline of Antarctica, which would throw the particular age of discovery back to a time before that coast was capped with its present cover of ice (not later than 4000 B.C.). This would place the beginnings of map making at least a thousand years before the earliest known writing. The Piri Reis map also shows with considerable accuracy the east coast of South America, and the eastern part of the Amazon.[77]

The Sea People were not limited to one ethnic or linguistic group, though their leadership may have tended to come from a special elite. However, the order within which they functioned required some conventions for communicating. The ecumene may well have recognized some form of sign language. In any case, Herodotus [78] tells how Phoenician (or, more precisely, Carthaginian) mariners traded with African natives: the Phoenicians would leave their wares on the beach and return to their ships; the natives would come, examine the merchandise, leave an amount of gold, and withdraw. The Phoenicians would then return to shore, count this gold, and, if not satisfied, go back to their ships. If the natives wished, it was their turn to add to the gold they were willing to pay. This could go on for an indefinite number of times, but the natives would not carry off the merchandise until the Phoenicians had taken the gold; nor would the Phoenicians take back their merchandise without leaving the gold behind. Thus without using spoken or written language, various people in the order could conduct business through conventional devices.

It is also probable that, in remote antiquity, the ecumene communicated through a lingua franca. The Bible reflects the use of a lingua franca in an incident that took place in 701 B.C. An Assyrian diplomat was requested by the Judean leaders not to speak in the Judean language but in the international Aramaic language so as to keep matters secret from the common people, who were listening.[79] In the Amarna Age (fifteenth to fourteenth centuries B.C.), Babylonian was the lingua franca, in which the Pharaohs corresponded not only with the Kings of Babylonia, but with Hittite, Canaanite, Hurrian and other non-Babylonian rulers. Thus the phenomenon of "lingua franca" was familiar to the Hebrews and other ancient Near Easterners, although they had no word for it.

Genesis 11 refers interestingly to an age of international builders. After the Flood (narrated in Genesis 7–8) talented men embarked on great projects such as the Tower of Babel, made possible through a common language with a conventional vocabulary ("one set of words"[80] in the original Hebrew of Genesis 11:1). The Hebrew author knows perfectly well that without a common language, international enterprise is impeded. With the breakdown of the lingua franca, the old international order broke down, so that each of the component people spoke only its own language and the great enterprise had to be abandoned. The text handles the crucial points with characteristic brevity, and the last thing we should do is blow up the sparse data into a vast hypothesis. We offer this new interpretation, because it fits the emerging pattern of ancient history, and is in keeping with the tendency of ancient traditions to preserve a kernel of historicity.

The first Sea People who are described as such in historic texts are the Minoans. They were in the East Mediterranean before 2000 B.C., and their dwindling remnants persisted into Hellenistic and perhaps into early Christian times. Their heyday was from about 1800 to 1400

B.C. Though based on Crete with their capital at Knossos, the Minoans had far-flung colonies on islands and continental points essential for maintaining their control of the seas. We know of eleven Minoan foundations in the East and Central Mediterranean called "Minoa." Gaza, one of them, is called "Gaza Minoa" on a Greek coin. Another Minoa is in Transjordan, where it apparently served as a midway station to link Minoan trade routes on the Mediterranean with those on the Red Sea.

Related to Minoan writing are specimens coming from various parts of the Mediterranean (from Anatolia to Iberia) [81] and beyond (including the Metcalf Stone from the U.S.A.). The evidence points in the direction of an ancient maritime system of which the Mediterranean was only a part, albeit an important part. This is reflected in the *Timaeus* of Plato, which tells of an exceedingly ancient Atlantic Order with interests extending from America into the Mediterranean. It is futile to dwell on the lost island of Atlantis (which Plato tells us sank 9,000 years earlier according to Egyptian hearsay passed on to Solon) and then to forget his plain reference to the continent that seals off the Atlantic Ocean on the West.[82] This continent—which Plato mentions without more ado because it was well known to his reading public— can only be America.

The Sea People—whom historians have hitherto considered as originating in and limited to the Mediterranean—ranged intercontinentally via oceanic as well as Mediterranean sea-lanes. It is no accident that Greek, Latin and Egyptian words are embedded in the languages of ancient Mesoamerica; that the feathered headdress on the Phaistos Disc warrior (worn also by the Philistines) is also common among the Indians of America; or that native Mesoamerican traditions attribute the impetus for their civilization to bearded white men who had sailed across the Atlantic from the Old World.

A group of Sea People bore the name of "Dan." The Bible tells how a segment of the seafaring (Judges 5:17) Danites won their way into the tribal system of ancient Israel (Judges 18–19). Early in the twelfth century B.C., the Danites were allies of their fellow Sea People the Philistines in assaulting Egypt during the reign of Ramses III, who fended them off, thus forcing them to concentrate on their more successful occupation of the Philistine Plain of the Pentapolis (Gaza,

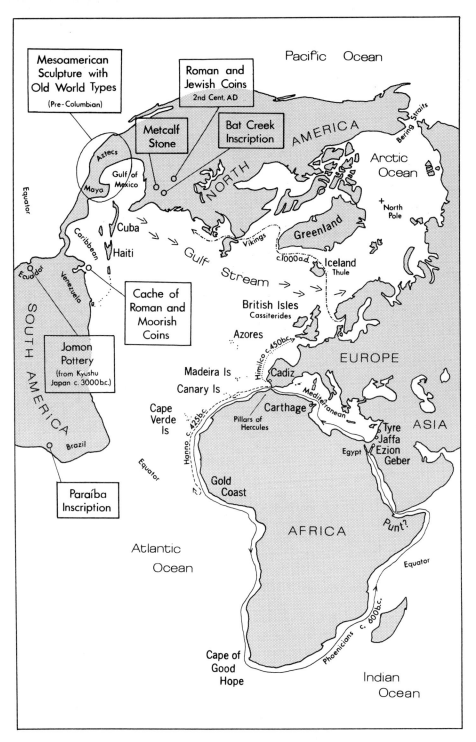

Pacific Ocean

Mesoamerican
Sculpture with
Old World Types
(Pre-Columbian)

Roman and
Jewish Coins
2nd Cent. AD

Metcalf
Stone

Bat Creek
Inscription

NORTH AMERICA

Arctic
Ocean

Bering Straits

+ North
Pole

Aztecs

Gulf of
Mexico

Maya

Equator

Cuba

Caribbean

Haiti

Vikings

Gulf Stream

Greenland

c.1000 a.d.

Iceland
Thule

Cache of
Roman and
Moorish
Coins

Ecuador

Venezuela

British Isles
Cassiterides

EUROPE

Azores

Himilco c.450 b.c.

SOUTH AMERICA

Jomon
Pottery
(from Kyushu
Japan c. 3000 b.c.)

Madeira Is

Canary Is

Cadiz

Mediterranean

ASIA

Cape
Verde
Is

Carthage

Pillars of
Hercules

Tyre
Jaffa

Egypt

Ezion
Geber

Brazil

Hanno c. 425 b.c.

Equator

Gold
Coast

Punt?

Paraíba
Inscription

AFRICA

Atlantic
Ocean

Equator

Phoenicians c. 600 b.c.

Cape of
Good
Hope

Indian
Ocean

TRANSATLANTIC ROUTES

Series of glazed tiles representing captives taken in the wars of Ramses III (early twelfth century B.C.*). Note the care taken to depict the physiognomies and clothing distinctively.* COURTESY, MUSEUM OF FINE ARTS, BOSTON

Ascalon, Ekron, Gath and Ashdod). The Danites were widespread. Cyprus was called Ia-Dnan "The Island of Dan(an)." The same people were called Danuna, and under this name they appear as rulers of the Plain of Adana in Cilicia. Greek tradition has their eponymous ancestor, Danaos, migrating from the Nile Delta to Greece where he became King of Argos. So important was this movement that the Greeks afterward called themselves Danaoi for centuries. Vergil also designated the Greeks as "Danai." Bold scholars see the influence of the Danites in Irish lore about the goddess Danu; and in the name of Danmark ("Denmark"): the land of Dan.

In any case, it is a mistake to accept the consensus and to imagine that Sea People with enough striking power in the twelfth century B.C. to change the course of history were unenterprising to the point of never sailing west of Gibraltar.

The language of the Minoans, Philistines and Danites was Northwest Semitic: within which fall Hebrew, Phoenician, Ugaritic, Aramaic and a variety of related dialects such as Moabite and Edomite.[83] The Hebrews called their language "the speech of Canaan"; and the Phoenicians refer to their land as Canaan and to themselves as Canaanites. The dialects which scholars now call "Canaanite" were all mutually intelligible; they include Hebrew, Phoenician, Moabite and Edomite.

Canaan had at its heart the Syro-Palestinian land bridge connecting Asia and Africa. It also had ports on the Mediterranean and Red seas. This is what made of Palestine the hub of ancient commerce: it was a crossroads of unique importance, with one set of routes joining the world's two largest continents, and another linking the Mediterranean and Atlantic waterways with those of the Red Sea and Indian Ocean. Abraham was part of a trading aristocracy that operated in Canaan for basic commercial reasons. It is significant that in Hebrew "Canaanite" designates not only a person from Canaan, but serves also as a common noun meaning "merchant."

The merchant mariners par excellence in the Bronze Age were the Minoans; in the Iron Age, the Phoenicians.[84] The two peoples are probably interconnected historically. When the Northwest Semitic Minoans had lost their grip on the Aegean, they had to take to their ships (in stages, for the process took time) and reestablish themselves in areas where they could protect themselves and their interests more effectively. By 1500 B.C., the Mycenaean Greeks were gaining the ascendancy in the Aegean, so that waves of Northwest Semites like the Phoenicians and Philistines were basing themselves on the coast of Canaan. By the Amarna Age (as we know from texts like the Ugaritic and Amarna tablets), the Phoenicians were in possession of Byblos, Sidon, Tyre and other ports along the Syro-Palestinian coast. At the same time the Philistines were active in southern Canaan. Fresh waves strengthened the earlier settlers from the Aegean so that as the Iron Age was inaugurated in the twelfth century, these Sea Peoples controlled most of the coast.

Biblical Israel was not homogeneous. Its amphictyonic system of twelve tribes embraced populations with different ways of life. Three of the tribes are described as navigational: Zebulun, Dan and Asher (Genesis 49:13; Judges 5:17). In *modus vivendi,* such ancient Israelites were more akin to Phoenicians and Philistines than to the inland Hebrews.

During the period of the Judges (twelfth and eleventh centuries B.C.), the Hebrews gradually fell under the domination of the technologically superior Philistines. The latter were warlords whose skill in metallurgy gave them a decisive advantage in the manufacture and maintenance of weapons. Indeed, through monopolizing the metal industry, they kept the Hebrews disarmed.[85] By 1000 B.C., Syria-Palestine consisted of a multitude of city-states unhampered by any world power. Mesopotamia, Anatolia, Egypt and the Aegean lacked the strength to take over or control the area. This provided ancient Israel with its opportunity to win a place in the sun.

King Saul united the Israelite tribes in the struggle for liberation against the Philistines. David, meanwhile, prepared himself for carrying on the struggle to a successful conclusion, by learning from the enemy. David and his troops entered the service of Achish, the Philistine king of Gath. There he mastered the art of war from the very people whose military superiority had kept the Hebrews in subjugation. When Saul's brave attempt ended in failure at the hands of the Philistines in the Battle of Gilboa, David emerged and carried on the struggle (ca. 1000 B.C.). A succession of victories not only liberated Israel from the Philistine yoke, but carved out an empire from the Egyptian border to the Euphrates River.

David's statesmanship evoked a program to create prosperity by combining land and sea power. Accordingly, he made an alliance with Hiram I of Tyre that was destined to last into the reign of his son Solomon. The pact enabled Israel to profit from Phoenician shipbuilding and navigational personnel and experience. Hiram benefited from Israel's control of the land routes (including caravan cities) and of access to the Red Sea via the key port of Ezion-geber. Herodotus tells us that the Phoenicians came from the Red Sea.[86] However we interpret the evidence, it is clear that the Phoenicians had prior mercantile interests and experience in the Indian Ocean via the Red Sea.[87]

The fleets sent out by Hiram and Solomon from Ezion-geber undertook long voyages including regularly scheduled missions that took up to three years for the round trip.[88] Ophir, rich in gold, was a source of wealth for Solomon.[89] Its location is still undetermined; but the fact that a text mentioning "gold of Ophir" has been found at Tell Qasile, on the Mediterranean coast of Israel, suggests that Ophir could be reached via Gibraltar as well as via the Red Sea, pointing to an Atlantic location of Ophir.[90] The Straits of Gibraltar were not always open to traffic from the East Mediterranean, for they could be closed by any rival sea power that controlled the West Mediterranean. Accordingly, Ezion-geber was not only important for Indian Ocean trade, but also for access to the Atlantic in case the Mediterranean exit was blocked.

Some of the products brought by the fleet of Hiram and Solomon suggest the identification of their lands of origin. Ivory and monkeys [91] could come from either Africa or India. If the translation of *tukkiyyîm* as "peacocks" is correct, India is indicated. The quest for metals, stones, special woods and other valued materials including ivory impelled the ancient merchant kings such as Hiram and Solomon to launch expeditions to the ends of the earth. The skills and drive were there. Naval architecture, along with celestial and other methods of navigation, had been refined, and exploration and cartography had gone through a long development. The advent of the Iron Age necessitated access to iron as well as to the metals of the Bronze Age: gold, silver, copper, tin and lead.

A distant land called Tarshish must have been located along the shores of the Atlantic, because it too could be reached via the Red Sea as well as via the Mediterranean.[92] It yielded silver, iron, tin and lead. Though Ophir had been developed by the South Arabians,[93] Tarshish had ancient ties with the Ionian Greeks.[94] These facts, embedded in Genesis 10, show that the ancient ecumene was not restricted to the Near East or Mediterranean, but extended to the distant parts of the earth through the sea-lanes. We shall later return to the avenues of approach for identifying Tarshish.

The commercial empires fostered a policy of establishing colonies to look after the interests of the homeland. The Minoans, as we have noted, left a trail of colonies called "Minoa." Later the Greek cities continued the pattern of sending out colonies. The Phoenicians were famous for this method of expansion. Tyre, for example, colonized Cyprus, founding cities like Kition and Larnaca, which in turn sent out colonies to Sardinia, as early as the ninth century B.C., and to Italy in the neighborhood of Rome.[95] Solomon settled Israelites at key points of his empire beyond the natural borders of Israel.[96] We may infer that he and Hiram did the same to look after their commercial interests in various parts of the world.[97] Indeed the Jewish Diaspora went hand in hand with the spread of Phoenician commerce. The disintegration of the Solomonic Empire in the second half of the tenth century B.C. cut the colonies of Israelites off from their homeland, though many of them maintained their Israelite identity, thus beginning the Jewish Diaspora.

The most powerful colony of the Phoenicians was Carthage, whose beginnings may go back to the twelfth century B.C., though its solid foundation is traditionally dated in 814 B.C. It gained control of the Central and West Mediterranean. In the fifth century B.C. it sponsored expeditions along the coasts of Europe and Africa. The European venture, led by Himilco around 450 B.C., is narrated in the *Ora Maritima* by the Latin poet Avienus. Hanno, as we read in the Greek translation of his log known as the *Periplus,* sailed through Gibraltar with a fleet of sixty ships carrying 30,000 people, and planted colonies along the west coast of Africa around 425 B.C.[98] Meanwhile Cadiz had been founded as early as the twelfth century B.C. (in 1110 B.C.) by the Phoenicians, as the first important historical city of Western Europe.

The divided kingdoms of Israel and Judah continued to embark, at least intermittently, on naval exploits out of Ezion-geber. King Ahab of Israel took as his queen the Tyrian princess Jezebel, strengthening

Hebraic ties with the Phoenicians. It is no accident that Ahab's son, Ahaziah, is described as taking the lead in urging Jehoshaphat of Judah to reactivate merchant marine expeditions out of Ezion-geber, during the ninth century B.C. (1 Kings 22:49), only now Israel rather than Tyre was the nautical partner of the House of David.

The Phoenicians did not lose their touch. Around 600 B.C., Pharaoh Necho II commissioned a Phoenician fleet to circumnavigate Africa, sailing down the east coast, rounding the Cape of Good Hope and returning to Egypt in the third year via Gibraltar (Herodotus 4:42).

The finest description of Phoenician seamanship and trade comes to us from the prophet Ezekiel (Chapter 27) during the early part of the sixth century B.C. Tyrian fleets intrepidly sailing the seven seas were bringing untold wealth from distant lands, including iron (Ezekiel 27:12, 19) from the far-off Atlantic land called Tarshish (v. 12).

In 539 B.C. came a turning point in history. Cyrus the Great of Persia toppled the Neo-Babylonian Empire and gained control of Western Asia up to the shores of the Mediterranean. The Phoenician cities had to come to terms with him and harmonize their interests with those of the new Achaemenian Empire. The Mediterranean, however, was divided between two spheres of power. The Carthaginians controlled the West, the Achaemenians the East Mediterranean. Thus the east Phoenicians, as members of the Achaemenian Order, were forced into the camp of the rivals and foes of Carthage. This obliged Carthage to keep the east Phoenicians out of the West Mediterranean, and block their access to the Atlantic.

The Phoenicians of Tyre and Sidon knew how to cope with the situation for they had reopened the Red Sea route to the Atlantic under the aegis of Necho at the dawn of the century (ca. 600 B.C.). Accordingly, Ezion-geber remained important. The probable site of that port is the little offshore island now called Jezirat Farᶜawn ("Pharaoh's Island") a few miles south of Elath, less than three hundred meters off the Sinai coast. It conforms to the Phoenician pattern of offshore island strongholds with port facilities like Arwad, ancient Tyre and Motya. One of the characteristic Phoenician features of Jezirat Farᶜawn is the *cothon* or man-made inner harbor, which happens to be almost exactly the same size as the *cothon* at Motya, in western Sicily.

In the sixth century B.C., during Early Iron Age III, the ecumene

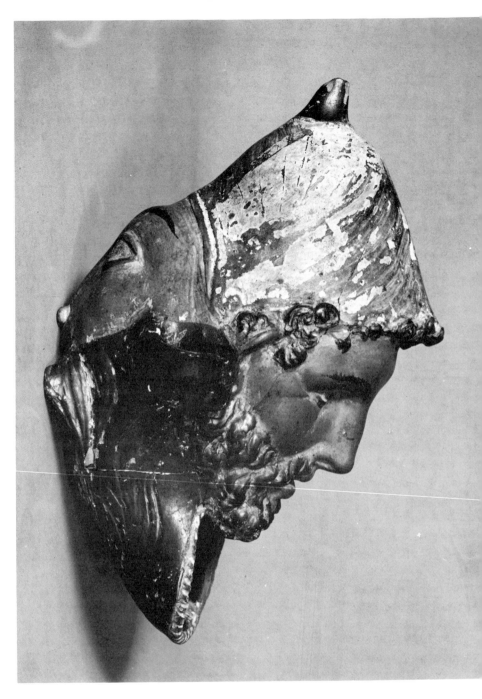

Etruscan rhyton of the fourth century B.C., *when the Achaemenian
Empire linked the Far East with Europe. On one side (a) is a
Classical European face, on the other (b) a Mongolian man from
the Far East.* COURTESY, MUSEUM OF FINE ARTS, BOSTON

a

b

Jezirat Farᶜawn ("Pharaoh's Island"): Site of Ezion-geber.

had to include major sources of iron. In the Bronze Age, three key areas bore names associated with the metals for which they were famous. Nubia, rich in gold, was connected with *nbw,* the Egyptian word for "gold." Hatus-, capital of the Hittite Empire, was written ideographically as SILVER city, and sounded like (if indeed it was not identical with) a word for "silver" now known in Ugaritic. Greek *kypros* designates "copper" as well as "Cyprus," the main source of copper in the ancient Near East. The word for "iron" in most of the Semitic languages, other than Arabic, is *barzel* (as the word appears in Hebrew). It is not of Semitic origin to judge by the atypical phonetic correspondences in the various Semitic languages (e.g., *bržl* in Ugaritic, *parzillu* in Akkadian). The word found its way into the Atlantic community, for in the Midland counties of England, *brazil* designates "iron pyrites." In the English idiom "hard as brazil" the meaning "iron" is smoother than the usual interpretation of "Brazil wood." [99] Old Irish lore refers to Hy Brasil "The Island of Brazil" out in the Atlantic beyond Ireland. This type of name is typically Phoenician; the name of the Balearic island Ibiza is derived from Phoenician *'î Bes* "The Island of Bes," and an old Phoenician name of Sardinia was *'î Nesîm* "The Island of Hawks." An able Hispanic and Semitic scholar, Joseph M. Solá-Solé, cites the suggestion that "Hispania" is of Semitic derivation and may stand for Phoenician *Hi-sapan* "The Island of the Rabbit." [100] In any case, the old Irish name of the land—or a land—in the West, is Hy Brasil which stands for Northwest Semitic *'î* BRZL "The Island of Iron."

Already, in the days of Columbus, West European explorers of the New World were seeking "the Island of Brazil" [101] with its legendary Seven Cities.[102] Whether "the Island of Brazil" designated a part of the country now known as Brazil has not yet been proved. We can however say that no country in the world merits the name BRZL "Iron" more than Brazil, whose chief resource is still iron. Indeed it is reported that 25 percent of the world's known iron reserves are in the Brazilian province of Minas Gerais.[103] Other parts of Brazil are also rich in iron, and the Manaus area along the Amazon is now being exploited for it. In any event, we can be sure that in the Iron Age, the ecumene expanded beyond the Bronze Age horizons of the Old World whose metal-bearing lands included golden Nubia, silver Anatolia and copper Cyprus. The Iron Age ecumene included an iron-rich "Brazil" somewhere out in the Atlantic—perhaps including some of modern Brazil. The latter possibility must be weighed in the light of an inscription, reported to have been found in Brazil in 1872, and, if authentic, records a crossing from Canaan to Brazil in 534–531 B.C.

On September 11, 1872, a person who signed "Joaquim Alves da Costa" wrote a letter to the Viscount of Sapucahy, President of the Instituto Historico, in Rio de Janeiro. Enclosed was a copy of a Canaanite inscription. The covering letter explained that the writer's slaves had found an inscribed stone on his plantation at Pouso Alto near Paraíba. The text seemed curious and important enough for Da Costa to transmit a facsimile to the scholars of the Instituto Historico.

A talented and enterprising member of the Instituto, Ladislau Netto, undertook the study of the document with a view to publishing it. The only person in Brazil with a reputation for familiarity with Semitic languages such as Hebrew and Arabic was at that time the Emperor Dom Pedro II. But even he was an amateur whose knowledge was by no means equal to the task of deciphering the Canaanite text. Netto plunged into the study of Hebrew and Phoenician with the intensity of a spirited pioneer. The outstanding authority on Canaanite epigraphy was then Ernest Renan, the French savant and man of letters, whose knowledge and reputation were exceeded only by his pedantry. The Emperor and Netto turned to the great Renan for guidance. Apparently Netto did not trust the character of the savant in Paris because instead of sending him the complete text for evaluation, Netto sent him only short selections, so that Renan could not scoop him. Renan informed his Brazilian correspondents that while no one should pronounce judgment on a text he has not seen, he was sure it was a forgery anyway. After misreading and misinterpreting passages that had been sent to him, Renan declared it a fake.

Brazil was then on the fringes of West European culture, and no one there had the temerity or knowledge to stand up against the leader of the European Establishment on learned matters such as Semitic inscriptions. Accordingly, Dom Pedro, overwhelmed by Renan, withdrew his support from Netto who had taken the text seriously and, by hard work, had translated enough of the inscription to know that it told of a crossing from Ezion-geber to Brazil in the sixth century B.C.

Some European scholars supported the authenticity of the text, others opposed it; but the consensus condemned it as spurious. A competent German Semitist, Konstantin Schlottmann, took the only reasonable position: open-mindedness. He showed that some items looked suspicious, while others gave every indication of being genuine. For this he was scorned by a more typical representative of the Establishment, Mark Lidzbarski.

It happens that the reasons for branding the text as a forgery have turned out to be wrong. Some were misreadings; others were unknown grammatical forms that have subsequently come to light during the century that has elapsed since 1872. But the spirit of negativism prevailed, as it normally does with an Establishment that lacks the flexibility to alter a generally accepted basic assumption. At the start of the nineteenth century, great intellectuals like Alexander von Humboldt had global perspective. During the latter decades of the century, the seeds of overspecialization and hypercriticism were producing the harvest of negativism from which the humanities are still suffering.

During the early months of 1874, Netto retained his faith in the text, despite the fact that every attempt to locate Da Costa had failed. Meanwhile Netto had become the target of ridicule, which was unbearable for a man of ability, station and pride. Lacking the technical knowledge to defend what he instinctively felt to be right, he eventually recanted in an open "Letter to Ernest Renan," hoping thereby to "get off the hook." If there are Seven Heavens, Renan's Heaven for Pedantic Savants lies far below Netto's Heaven for Men of Vision. But there ought to be a still higher Heaven for Men of Vision who do not succumb to the cruel smallness of the world about them.

I had for many years been aware of the Brazil text through a badly garbled copy that left me with mixed feelings. In no case did I intend to get involved with a suspect document known to me only through a transcription I did not trust. So I kept the matter, along with other curiosa, in the back of my mind. A chance visit to Mexico City in 1959 had provided me with an opportunity to observe so many pre-Columbian monuments with so many interlocked connections with the Old World, that I have ever since been inclined to posit ancient contacts between the Eastern and Western Hemispheres. All this prepared me for an unexpected turn of events in November 1967.

From 1946 to 1956, I lived in Princeton, N.J. During those years I met a graduate student, Jules Piccus, who was preparing for the doctorate in Hispanic Studies. He realized the importance of Semitic languages in understanding the fabric of Spanish and Portuguese civilization. The Phoenicians, Jews and Arabs have left such an indelible impression on the Iberian Peninsula that without knowing their roles it is impossible to fathom the character of the Spanish and Portuguese people. Piccus kept up an interest in Semitics and consulted me on the subject from time to time. We had not corresponded or seen each other for a number of years, when suddenly I got a small parcel of documents from him, with a covering letter dated November 22, 1967.

Dr. Piccus, now a Professor of Hispanic Studies at the University of Massachusetts at Amherst, informed me that he had acquired a scrapbook about the Brazilian Stone with a new copy of the text, and a covering letter dated January 31, 1874, sent from Rio by Ladislau Netto to Wilberforce Eames in New York City. The scrapbook was apparently put together and bound by Wilberforce Eames (who later became the Librarian of the New York Public Library). Piccus had purchased the scrapbook for a small sum at a rummage sale in Providence, R.I.

Piccus investigated the problem as best he could before consulting me. He had the acumen to see that Renan's judgment was based on misreadings. He also facilitated my initial research by providing me with Xeroxed copies not only of the whole scrapbook, but of some pertinent nineteenth-century articles. My conclusion that the text is genuine is based on the fact that it contains readings unknown in 1872 but which are now authenticated by inscriptions discovered during the century that has elapsed since then. To deny this means crediting a forger with the clairvoyance to anticipate a hundred years of discovery in a highly technical field: an alternative that no rational person who knows the facts of the case should elect.

The Da Costa letter of September 11, 1872, to the President of the Instituto Historico, runs as follows in English translation:

"Mr. Viscount,
"As I was having stones moved on my property of Pouso Alto near Parahyba,[104] my slaves brought me one which they had already broken into four pieces. That stone bore numerous characters which no one

understood. I had them copied by my son who knows a bit of draughts-manship, and I decided to send this copy to Your Excellency, as President of the Historic and Geographic Institute of Brazil, to see whether Your Excellency or someone else can find out what these letters mean. Since I have come to the capital and have not the time to deliver them personally to Your Excellency, I am mailing them to him.

"I am with complete consideration and respect

"Your Excellency's

"Attentive, devoted and obliged servant

"Joaquim Alves da Costa

"Rio, 11 September 1872"

Netto, who correctly evaluated the importance of the inscription, took every possible step to locate Pouso Alto and Da Costa, but in vain. There are quite a number of Pouso Altos in Brazil, and there were even more of them in 1872. Moreover, there are two Paraíba's: (1) the Province of Paraíba in the north, jutting farther east than any other part of continental America; and (2) the region of Paraíba (along the Paraíba River) in the south, closer to Rio de Janeiro. The southern Paraíba is the more likely area because it is closer to Rio and to the iron mines of Minas Gerais (via the Paraíba River) which would be a logical goal of the ancient mariners. Besides, the Province of Paraíba was rather far away for a business visit to Rio back in 1872.

It is of course possible that "Joaquim Alves da Costa" is a pseudonym used by a person who possessed the stone and did not want it confiscated by the State because of its importance. Perhaps he submitted it to the Instituto out of purely scientific motives; or perhaps he wanted a free and publicized evaluation that would enhance the value and raise its price.

It is idle to speculate on such matters. Strange things happen, and this is not more bizarre than the discovery of the Dead Sea Scrolls by a goat pursued by an illiterate Arab shepherd. Even today, when there are many organized expeditions, a large proportion of the important discoveries are made by chance. It was a crew working for building contractors who accidentally dug into the Palace of Cadmus at Thebes and found a large collection of Babylonian seal cylinders. To the average classicist, Babylonian inscriptions on seals from Thebes are as far out as a Canaanite text from Brazil is to the average Semitist. Nor is it unusual for genuine inscriptions of great importance to get lost, remaining known only through copies. Copies of the Eteocypriote-Greek bilingual from Amathys, Cyprus, have been published, but the original stone is lost.

The state of affairs early in 1874 is described in Ladislau Netto's letter to Wilberforce Eames, which we translate from Netto's French:

"31 January 74

"My dear sir:

"It is only now that I am able to answer the letter by which you honored me in writing during July of last year. Before writing to you I tried to get some positive data for you about the Phoenician monument which I know only from the copy of which I am sending you the attached facsimile with translations into Hebrew and French regardless of the inaccuracies in them. Unfortunately, in spite of the official and private steps which I have taken to locate the person who sent us the copy of the monument, I have no news of him. If it is a ruse, I cannot detect what prompted it, for nearly two years have passed since that manuscript was sent to the Historical Institute of Brazil, and up to now, nobody has claimed to be its author. Furthermore, the dispatch was made under such natural circumstances that no one suspected a mystery.

"Accept, sir, the assurance of my most respectful sentiments.

"Ladislau Netto
"Director of the National Museum"

Here is my translation of the eight-line inscription:

"We are Sidonian Canaanites from the city of the Merchant King. We were cast (2) up on this distant island, a land of mountains. We sacrificed a youth to the celestial gods (3) and goddesses in the nineteenth year of our mighty King Hiram (4) and embarked from Eziongeber into the Red Sea. We voyaged with ten ships (5) and were at sea together for two years around Africa. Then we were separated (6) by the hand of Baal and were no longer with our companions. So we have come here, twelve (7) men and three women, into "Island of Iron.""

Am I, the Admiral, a man who would flee? (8) Nay! May the celestial gods and goddesses favor us well!"

The text as a whole follows a tripartite format for commemorative historic Northwest Semitic inscriptions, unknown in 1872 but now fully attested. It consists of three parts: (1) the identification of the subject(s), (2) the event(s) commemorated, and (3) an appeal to the gods. In 1947 a commemorative Northwest Semitic text following this format was found at Karatepe, Cilicia (in Turkey).

The component elements also ring true, ranging from the date formula to the specification of a sacrifice.[105]

This is the first known text from the Red Sea navy. It is therefore not surprising that it contains some unusual expressions. The feminine gender of *'iy* "island" is attested only once in the Bible in a passage that only a subtle Hebrew grammarian would notice.[106]

The negated verb (line 6) *wl' nh* (pronounced $w^e l\bar{o}\ n^e h\bar{\imath}$) "and we were not" (or "and we were no longer . . .") was not recognized in the Hebrew Bible until 1968 when, as a result of this inscription, it was detected in Job 23:11. It could hardly be the work of a forger in 1872.

In line 3, the numeral "19" (*tš°t w°šrt*) was used in the nineteenth century as evidence against the authenticity of text because the suffix *-t* attached simultaneously to the digit and the ten was unheard of in Northwest Semitic until 1957 when other examples from Ugaritic were published in profusion.

The expression "hand of Baal" to indicate "fate" or "divine will" went unrecognized in the nineteenth century, but in 1939 it turned up in a Phoenician inscription from Cyprus.

The script cannot be earlier than the sixth century B.C., which rules out Hiram I (tenth century B.C.) and Hiram II (who paid tribute to Tiglath-Pileser III around 738 B.C.). The king can only be Hiram III (553–533 B.C.) so that the voyage from Ezion-geber began in 534, and ended in Brazil in 531. As noted above, this took place at a period when the Near East was under Achaemenian rule, and Gibraltar was controlled by the Carthaginian rivals of Cyrus the Great. The historical setting explains why the fleet sailed from Ezion-geber, taking the long (but open) way to the Atlantic.

The first person plural pronominal suffix *-nā* agrees with Arabic and Aramaic, against Hebrew and Phoenician *-nū*. Ezion-geber is in full view of the northwest coast of Arabia which has long been populated by Arabic-speaking tribes (though it is also true that some Arameans had settled in the vicinity). It happens that the *crux interpretum* in the text can be explained through Arabic usage, though the root of the word in question occurs also in Hebrew. In line 7, the land where the ship landed is called "The Island of ḤDT" which, as it stands, makes no sense in familiar Hebrew or Phoenician. *Ḥadd* (fem. *ḥaddat*) means "sharp" in Hebrew and can be applied to metal swords. But it is in Arabic that the root specifically designates "iron" (*ḥadîd* is the normal word for "iron" in Arabic). An Arabism is not strange in a text emanating from the Gulf of Aqaba Fleet, and in which the pronoun has affinities with Arabic against standard Canaanite. "Island of Iron" is also the meaning of Hy Brasil "The Island of Brazil" (connected with BRZL "iron" so plentiful in the New World, especially in Brazil).

We do not need this text for proving that Old World mariners reached the shores of America centuries and even millennia before Columbus. Its importance lies rather in providing us with a specific contact at a definite time by people who have recorded the event in a historic text.

The crossing was probably not an accident like the discovery of Brazil by the Portuguese navigator Pedro Alvares Cabral, who was blown across the Atlantic from Africa to Brazil in 1500 A.D., contrary to his plan to sail around the Cape of Good Hope to India. The winds and currents are all in favor of east-to-west crossings at that latitude where the Atlantic happens also to be much narrower than it is in the Northern Hemisphere between Europe and America. There is every reason to believe that the ship that reached Brazil in 531 B.C. sailed intentionally to a land (already known to the Canaanites by its name "Island of Iron") to get raw materials for the homeland as vividly described by Ezekiel (Chapter 27); the Hebrew prophet who in that sixth century B.C. described what was then going on.

The expression "from the hand of Baal" could be interpreted to mean "by a storm," but it more probably implies that this one ship was designated by lot to proceed to the Island of Iron,[107] while the other nine ships headed for other Atlantic ports within the network interconnected via the Red Sea Fleet.

To some, it may come as a surprise that sailors from the Near East reached America as early as 531 B.C. Actually that crossing occurred rather late in the history of Atlantic crossings by the ancient Sea People.

Chapter VII

THE EVIDENCE
OF LANGUAGE

GEOGRAPHY IS THE KEY to the high pre-Columbian achievements in Mesoamerica, for it is there that the Pacific and Atlantic coasts converge, exposing the area to simultaneous migrations from the east and west. By way of contrast, the U.S.A. and Canada cover terrain remote from both oceans, with the exception of the eastern and western fringes open to only one ocean. Cultural flowering is produced by the creative combination of different peoples, each with something significant to contribute. Western civilization, in the traditional sense, embodies the cultures of Israel, Greece and Rome—all of which in turn absorbed, in varying proportions, the contributions of Mesopotamian, Egyptian, various Indo-European and other peoples who preceded them, or who interacted with them as contemporaries. The Mediterranean is a sea that connected lands creatively; Middle America is a land that connected oceans creatively. The American Indian languages preserve traces of various Old World languages brought to these shores by ancestors from both the east and west.

Speech is a universal characteristic of humanity. Languages, like races, differ; but the importance of language in human affairs is such that influential groups of people leave linguistic traces behind them. Linguistics is an elaborate field that can be approached descriptively, historically or comparatively. Every language has its phonetics, morphology, syntax and lexicon. The scientific study of language is the most exact of the humanities, and sometimes approximates the precision of the natural sciences.[108]

For present purposes, the reader must bear in mind two different kinds of linguistic relationship. The first is genetic: when languages are descended from a common ancestor. This is the situation in the Romance languages, with Portuguese, Spanish, French, Italian, Romanian, etc. derived essentially from Vulgar Latin. The second is linguistic alliance, stemming from the fusing of languages that results from different linguistic groups living together. English is primarily Teutonic (for both the Angles and the Saxons were Teutonic) with a strong overlay of Norman French inaugurated by William the Conqueror. In English we find alongside Anglo-Saxon words like "brother, cook, sheep, cow," etc., Norman French words like "friar, chef, mutton, beef," etc.[109] Even grammatical elements have crept into English from Norman French, such as final -*s* to designate the plural. (Other plurals, as in "children, oxen, mice, geese, men, women," are Anglo-Saxon.) If the Norman French impact had been five times as strong as it was in fact, English would have been a Romance language with an Anglo-Saxon substratum.

No people is pure racially or linguistically. Creative peoples, and the languages they speak, are the results of felicitous combinations. The peoples of pre-Columbian America confront us with great variety racially [110] and linguistically. The diversity comes from countless combinations of people who crossed over to America via the Bering Straits as well as via many transoceanic sea-lanes at different latitudes during various periods from the Early Stone Age to the Renaissance.

Obviously, reconstructing the linguistic history of the New World is an enormous task still in its crude beginnings. And yet a start must be made. Our aim is to examine a balanced sampling of linguistic elements in order to set the subject on its correct course.

The historic framework within which we shall operate is one of internationalism, without any undue emphasis on any one people or linguistic group. We shall start with Mesopotamia. The *Euphrates* is the Greek form of the name of the Mesopotamian river that first appears in Sumerian in the form now read *Buranun(u)* by Sumerologists. Hebrew (*P^{e}rā-t* (with f. sg. suffix -*t*) "Euphrates" originally meant "river" because *Han-Nahar* "the River" in Hebrew is another way of designating the Euphrates. This suggests that the frequency of *para(n)* in the many river names of South America (Para, Paraíba, Paraná,

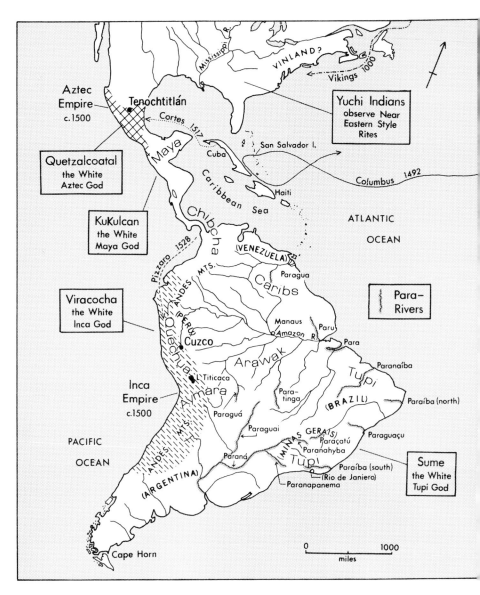

Aztec
Empire
c.1500

Tenochtitlán

Cortes 1517

Maya

VINLAND?

Vikings 1000

Mississippi

Yuchi Indians
observe Near
Eastern Style
Rites

Quetzalcoatal
the White
Aztec God

Cuba

San Salvador I.

Caribbean Sea

Haiti

Columbus 1492

KuKulcan
the White
Maya God

Pizzaro 1528

Chibcha

(VENEZUELA)

Paragua

ATLANTIC

OCEAN

Viracocha
the White
Inca God

ANDES MTS.

(PERU)

Quechua

Cuzco

Caribs

Manaus

Amazon R.

Paru

Para

Para-
Rivers

Arawak

Para

Inca
Empire
c.1500

L.Titicaca

Aymara

Para-
tinga

Paraguá

Paranaíba

Tupi

(BRAZIL)

Paraíba (north)

PACIFIC

OCEAN

ANDES MTS.

(ARGENTINA)

Paraguai

Paraná

MINAS GERAIS)

Paraçatú

Parañahyba

Tupi

Paraguaçu

Paraíba (south)

(Rio de Janiero)

Paranapanema

Sume
the White
Tupi God

Cape Horn

0   1000
miles

PRE-COLUMBIAN AMERICA

Paranaíba, Paranapanema, Paraguá, Paraguai, etc.) perpetuate the word for "river" brought in remote antiquity to South America by mariners linguistically akin to those who named the Euphrates. Mariners are interested in the rivers of the lands they discover and develop, for it is via the rivers that they penetrate the area. It is interesting to note that the Piri Reis map records South [111] but not North America realistically. The fact that the rivers beginning with "Para-" are in South but not North America suggests that the civilization responsible for exploring and mapping South America in remote antiquity (not later than 4000 B.C.) spoke the language in which *para* meant "river." The same people apparently explored Mesopotamia and bequeathed the name of the Euphrates in pre-Sumerian times (ca. 4000 B.C.?).

Another kind of link between Mesopotamia and Mesoamerican cultures is the seal cylinder. Cylindrical seals are the most characteristic small objects of Sumero-Akkadian civilization. Eventually the main use of the seal cylinder was for rolling on clay tablets while still wet, to serve as a signature. No two seals are the same any more than the fingerprints of any two people. Every person of consequence in ancient Mesopotamia had his distinctive seal for authenticating documents. However, there were other uses for seal cylinders. For example, large storage jars or even whole storage rooms could be sealed with clay impressed with a cylinder. The unbroken sealing served as legal proof that the contents had not been tampered with.

In Middle America there are many seal cylinders with pattern designs resembling those on early types of Mesopotamian seal cylinders of geometric and "brocade" styles. Cylindrical seals (as distinct from stamp seals) were designed for continuous rollings, as on fabrics for imprinting a painted design. Another use of the seal cylinder is to color a design on the human body: to produce the temporary effect of tattooing. This was practiced in Middle America with both stamp and cylindrical seals. Indeed there are concave American stamp seals specially curved for impressing the convex surfaces of the body. This at last explains the concavity of certain early Mesopotamian seal cylinders.[112] Like their American counterparts, they too were curved for imprinting their emblems on the body. Inasmuch as the early seals include many with heraldic [113] designs, they strengthen the theory of Svein-Magnus Grodys that conquerors carried their "coats of arms" with them in their victorious migrations.

(a) Hittite seal cylinder; (b) with stamp seal base; (c) Scene made by rolling the cylinder. The rolled scene is complex, but of special interest is the human sacrifice taking place at the upper right. The twisted rope and spiral designs are characteristic of the Sea People who formed an integral part of the Minoans. COURTESY, MUSEUM OF FINE ARTS, BOSTON

a

b

c

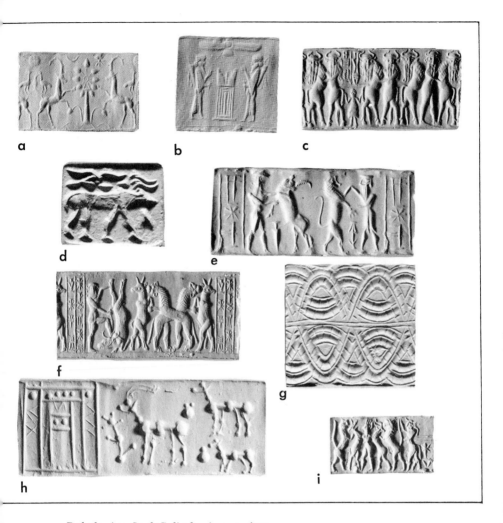

Babylonian Seal Cylinder impressions.
a. Animals flanking stylized tree. Late second millennium B.C.
b. Persian warriors flanking an altar, over which is the winged
symbol of Ahuramazda (ca. fifth century B.C.).
c, e, f. Heroes contending with animals and mythological beasts.
Dynasty of Akkad (ca. twenty-fourth century B.C.).
d. Stamp seal (ca. 3500 B.C.).
g. Pattern style design. Early Dynastic, first half of third millennium B.C.
h. Domestic animals and barn. Jemdet Nasr Period (ca. 3000 B.C.).
i. Heroes contending with animals. Early Dynastic (ca. 2500 B.C.).

Cylinder Seal from Tlatilco (Mexico) with stylized writing.
MILWAUKEE PUBLIC MUSEUM
PHOTOGRAPH

Cylindrical and Stamp Seals in the Guatemala City Museum.

In the light of the preceding discussion, *para* "river" is not an isolated link between Mesopotamia and ancient America, but fits into a broad cultural context.[114]

The ancients often transported live animals and plants from place to place by ship. Perhaps the best known example is Solomon's importation of monkeys and peacocks through his oceangoing fleet. Whether the geographical spread of the crocodile is due to human activity is to be determined by zoologists, but the fact is that not only the animal but also its name is distributed over the Old and New Worlds. In Egypt the crocodile was called *sbk* (usually pronounced *sobek*) and was worshiped in the Fayyum, which was the Crocodile Nome (= District). Now the Aztec name for the crocodile is *cipactli* whose stem is *cipac-* (pronounced *sipac-*) plus the nominal suffix *-tli*. As far as the consonants go, there is no discrepancy between Egyptian *sbk* and Nahuatl[115] *spk* because in the latter *b* and *p* are not distinguished.

The fact that the animal and its name are the same in Egypt and Middle America is striking enough, but we can go further. In both places the crocodile was worshiped both in its complete animal form or with certain human attributes. In the Mayan city of Tikal, a bone of the Late Classical Period (ca. A.D. 700) bears a carving that portrays a boat manned by three Mayans: one in the center, another at the prow and the third at the stern. They are transporting four seated animal deities; the last is crocodile-like (= an iguana?).[116] The carved scene is interesting in several ways, for it not only illustrates the worship of an assortment of zoomorphic gods, so typical of Egypt, but it also shows that sacred barks for the ceremonial transportation of gods were known in Middle America as well as on the Nile.

Religion is often very conservative, and there is every reason to believe that we are dealing here with deep-seated institutions, as persistent as the Cross throughout two millennia of Christian history. But the significance of the boat scene does not end here. Mayan studies, like Biblical studies until quite recently, operate on the tacit assumption that the culture was monopolized by landlubbers. This is belied not only by Mayan art such as the carved bone under discussion, but by the prominence of seashells among the finds in Mayan excavations. Most significant are the Mayan ports on both oceans, of which we may single out Tulum and Jaina on the coasts of Yucatán.

The linguistic equation of "American *cipac(tli)* = Egyptian *sbk*" is not isolated. It was in Egypt that monumental stone architecture was developed. In fact Imhotep, the architect of the Step Pyramid at Saqqara during the Early Bronze Age, is credited with inventing and implementing the idea. If one visits Chichén Itzá one is struck by the Step Pyramid (called the Castillo) built of stone and adorned with hieroglyphic inscriptions. Not far off is the Temple of the Warriors with its "forest of columns," of a piece with Egyptian hypostyle architecture. Moreover the Mayan and Egyptian calendars consist of 360 days plus five intercalary days that are not included in the monthly structure of the year. *S(p/b)k* thus links Mesoamerica and the Nile within a framework of interlocking parallels.

In Teletzinco Nahuatl, *wa* means "and" as in Semitic.[117] For reasons of internal Egypto-Semitic linguistics, we know that an earlier form was **iwa*. Again quite independent of Nahuatl evidence, final *-n* is sometimes suffixed, so that a complete form in Egypto-Semitic would be **iwan* identical with regular Nahuatl *iwan* "and" (often spelled, in Spanish fashion, *ihuan*). Sooner or later Old World philology will have to reckon with linguistic phenomena from the New World.[118]

The Indo-European impact on Middle America is evident even at the grammatical level. Thus an initial vowel (called "augment" by Indo-Europeanists) appears in Nahuatl.[119] Sometimes it is hard to tell which Indo-European language is responsible for loans in Nahuatl. For example *teo-tl* "god" could have been introduced from Greek *theo-s* or Latin *deu-s*. The Greek is more likely because of combinations like *teo-calli* "god's house" = "shrine," which Alexander von Humboldt correctly compared over a century and a half ago with Greek *theoû* "god's" + *kaliá* "house, shrine." [120]

Greek influence in ancient America does not come as a complete surprise. Since Mycenaean times, the Greeks have been a nautical people. No important Greek city was far from the sea, or lacked a port. Athens has its Piraeus, and Sparta its Gythion. That the Greeks had Atlantic connections is evident not only from classical authors,[121] but also from Genesis 10:4, as we shall soon note.

The Bible tells us that the distant land of Tarshish—rich in silver, iron, tin and lead (Ezekiel 27:12)—could be reached from the Mediterranean port of Jaffa (Jonah 1:3) or the Red Sea port of Ezion-geber (2 Chronicles 20:36).[122] A glance at the map tells us that the only part of the world that one would reach by ship from either the Mediterranean or Red Sea ports is the Atlantic seaboard. Tarshish, which must therefore lie on the shores of the Atlantic, is associated with Greek expansionism in Genesis 10:4, which states that Tarshish stems from Javan (*Yawan* in Hebrew, the eponymous ancestor of the Ionian Greeks). Mexico, rich in silver and other metal ores, is a possible identification of Tarshish—particularly in the light of the presence of Greek words in Nahuatl, though other Atlantic areas are not ruled out.

Latin words are also found.[123] Thus *papalotl* ("butterfly") resembles Latin *papilio* "butterfly." Nahuatl *mez-tli* "moon, month" has been compared with Latin *mensis*. Sometimes we are confronted with alternative possibilities; thus Nahuatl *tlalli* "land" might correspond to either *terra* or to *tellus* in Latin, for *r* and *l* fall together in Nahuatl.

The transoceanic mariners who came to ancient America arrived from many places and during many periods. That visitors came from Japan to the shores of Ecuador around 3000 B.C. does not exclude sailors from China, Southeast Asia and India via the Pacific. The fact that Phoenicians, Egyptians, Mesopotamians, Greeks, Etruscans and Romans may have reached various parts of the New World at different times does not rule out still others from the Near East and Mediterranean. Some ancient seafarers were more prominent than others in the process of discovery and development, but no one people monopolized the scene. It was rather the multiplicity of peoples that came to Mesoamerica that gave the area its boundless dynamism. To this day, Middle America is among the most naturally tolerant parts of the world, largely because from the start it has been the meeting ground of many races speaking many languages. Cultural, racial and linguistic give-and-take has been the norm there for thousands of years.

The phonetics of Nahuatl has a bearing on the character of the Aegean syllabary. In Linear A and B (and the Egyptian hieroglyphic system as well), *l* and *r* are not distinguished. This spelling habit stems from a linguistic community in which the two sounds had fallen together, such as the Aztec and Maya dialects. Ultimate Far Eastern influence is suggested by the fact that *r* and *l* fall together also in Chinese and Japanese. Note too the convergence of *p* and *b* in Nahuatl as well as in the Aegean syllabary. Minoan and Mycenaean civilizations confront us with problems whose solution requires an awareness of the links between the Old and New Worlds in remote antiquity.

Geographical names in America tell an important story, as brought out by John Philip Cohane in *The Key* (Crown Publishers, 1969). We have seen how "Brazil" is related to the word for "iron" in a number of Semitic languages; and how the South American river names beginning with "Para-" are linguistically related to the "Euphrates." We must not overlook evidence from other areas.[124] George Michanowsky has explored a subtributary of the Amazon east of the Andes, called "Khaweera Kelkata," which means "The River of Writing" in the native Aymara language. The name was apparently given to the river because of the petroglyphs that Michanowsky has located along the banks. Michanowsky makes the interesting suggestion that *kelka* (which means "writing" in Aymara) is akin to Sanskrit *kalikha* "*ka* writing"; the script of India in which *ka* is the first letter (for *likh* designates "writing").

Fortunately, there are thriving and conservative communities of Indians in Middle America. Millions of Aztecs and Mayans still speak their ancestral tongues. Now is the time for scholars to master the spoken Mayan dialects together with the intricacies of the Mayan inscriptions.[125] It is only by combining both lines of evidence—oral and written—that the riddle of the ancient Mayan texts will be solved. At present only the dates and some other expressions are clear. Reliance on machine techniques has not produced the results vainly expected by our materialistic society. In such matters, more confidence can be placed in individuals who personally control all the essential elements of information. Old Persian was cracked by one man: Georg Grotefend; the Cypriote syllabary, by George Smith; Linear B, by Michael Ventris. It will be qualified individuals rather than committees or teams who will convert the mysteries of the pre-Columbian inscriptions into the plain text from which history can be reconstructed.

Chapter VIII

CULTURAL TRANSMISSION

C U L T U R A L   E L E M E N T S are never borrowed unchanged. Indeed the changes are often so great that they obscure the borrowed essence.

Cultic mushroom stones are common in Middle America. Ordinarily they consist of a "stem and button" set on a tripod, all carved out of one stone about a foot and a half high. Dr. Dennis W. Lou, Professor of History at the State University of New York (Oneonta, N.Y.), has compared the American mushroom stones with the ancestor stones of his native China. The form was apparently suggested by the resemblance of the mushroom to a penis representing the male ancestor. Dr. Lou rightly maintains that ancestor worship makes more sense than mushroom worship,[126] and his view is substantiated by a series of mushroom stones in the Archeological and Ethnological Museum in Guatemala City. One of those stones has a man's face on the "stem," confirming Lou's theory that the stones stand for people. Another stone in the museum has a whole human head instead of the mushroom "stem," so that the "button" of the mushroom looks like a turban on the ancestor's head.

That ancestor worship fits into the Mayan scheme is confirmed by living Mayan usage. In Chichicastenango, Guatemala, Mayan Indians pray to their ancestors in the church under the aegis, not of the Catholic priests, but of their own witch doctors. On little platforms set up in the aisles of the church, they light single candles for female ances-

Mushroom Stones in the Archeological Museum, Guatemala City.

tors, and double candles for male ancestors. Rose petals are spread and liquor sprinkled to propitiate the ancestral spirits.

It is interesting that it took a Chinese scholar (Lou), familiar with the phenomenon of ancestor worship, to detect this link between Middle America and the Far East. This transpacific connection is not isolated. Indeed one of the oldest carbon-14 dated archeological connections between the Old and New Worlds is, as we have already noted, the Jomon pottery from Ecuador derived from Japan around 3000 B.C.

Now for a Near East connection with the New World. The smoking habit was touched off in Europe by the introduction of tobacco from America after the voyages of Columbus. Among the Indians, however, the smoking of tobacco was not a habit but a ritual. The place of the peace pipe in American Indian life was quite different from the use of pipes, cigars and cigarettes today. And yet there is no question that modern smoking is derived from a pre-Columbian American rite. Stone pipes were used ritually in the ancient Near East. Such pipes consist of a bowl and stem carved out of one stone. Some have animal heads on the bowl, and some have a hand (with all five fingers) carved in relief on the bottom of the bowl.[127]

It is interesting to note that American Indian pipes sometimes have animal or human heads carved on the bowl, as well as hands with all five fingers carved beneath the bowl.[128] The heads indicate that the bowls were personified, while the hands not only suggest that the fragrant smoke was being offered,[129] but also that the whole cultic object was called a "hand" (*kaf* "hand" is the name of such an object in Hebrew).

Since such smoking bowls appear during Old Testament times in the Near East, it is possible that the American peace pipes are an adaptation of Near East *kaf* pipes. They could have been introduced by Canaanites like those who reached America in 531 B.C. or by later visitors like the Mediterranean merchant prince of about A.D. 300 from Iximché in the Guatemalan province of Chimaltenango. The substitution of tobacco for Near East incense is a common type of transformation; i.e., the employment of what is available locally instead of an ingredient too difficult to import from afar. The ritual use of copal in America seems to be a simple "translation" of frankincense and other fragrant smokes used to propitiate the gods in the Old World.

The copal tree is native to Middle America. Tobacco, however, like so many plants discovered in America by Columbus and his successors, was transplanted in the Old World. The smoking habit transformed the very nature of the ancient American peace pipe from a solemn rite to a habit for personal gratification with no religious significance. Accordingly modern smoking is derived directly from the American peace pipe but ultimately from the Near East *kaf*.[130]

It is often difficult to see transformations, particularly in banal, everyday usages. Eating bread is so widespread that we tacitly assume it is a universal characteristic of all humanity. Yet this is not so, for even an old, highly refined cuisine, the south Chinese—whose Cantonese cooking is justly famed—lacks any form of bread. Anyone familiar with Near East bread (such as Arabic *khubz*) cannot help being struck with the similarity of the *tortillas* made of maize flour in Middle America. Accordingly, it is possible that Old World immigrants accustomed to bread made from wheat, barley, rye or other Old World grain flours "translated" bread into *tortillas* of native maize, from which they ground a flour and baked bread. Since America lacked all the grains familiar in the Old World, human ingenuity found a native substitute.

The wheel in pre-Columbian America was restricted to toy wagons as far as archeological study now records. The lack of draught animals may have ruled out the use of wheeled vehicles for practical purposes, but it is wrong to say that pre-Columbian Americans were ignorant of the wheel.

In the Andes the native llama and alpaca were used as pack animals for carrying burdens. The impression those small beasts make on visitors used to seeing sturdy Old World beasts of burden (such as camels, oxen, horses, mules or donkeys) is that they are more akin to sheep and goats than to real pack animals. Indeed they are not capable of carrying loads comparable with those a normal donkey can transport. We may accordingly be confronted with another example of translation. Old World people used to pack animals, on coming to the Andes, trained the little cameloids to carry burdens, not because they are well suited for that role, but because they were the best available substitute.

Since strange coincidences happen every day, it would be an error to insist that a similar feature in two parts of the world must be due to

*Statuette of Egyptian woman grinding grain to make flour. From
Giza, Fifth Dynasty (ca. 2300* B.C.*).* COURTESY, MUSEUM OF FINE
ARTS, BOSTON

diffusion. Isolated details may prove little or nothing *in any specific case,* though cumulatively a thousand such details might prove much. However, the evidence for diffusion grows when an intricate complex, with numerous interlocking details, is involved. The extraction of metals by smelting ore might, in two widely spread cases, be due to independent development. But when we find in pre-Columbian America the sophisticated *cire perdue* ("lost wax") method of casting, long known in the Old World, it is more difficult to deny cultural diffusion. As the technological details increase, it becomes harder to attribute the host of close similarities to the supposed universal oneness of the human mind.[131] Neither psychology nor anthropology nor the history of technology point to any "law" that can through independent invention explain the weaving of cotton fabrics in the Old and New Worlds.

Botanists assure us that American cotton, characterized by thirteen large plus thirteen small chromosomes, is the product of hybridizing the wild native American plant with Old World cotton such as was grown in ancient Egypt. The Old World variety could not have reached America by northern Viking routes because the cold kills it; nor could it have floated with the currents across the ocean because water kills it; nor could it have been carried by birds because they will not touch the cotton boll that contains the seeds. The Old World variety must have been brought dry, aboard ship, via warm sea-lanes.[132]

For weaving cotton, the plant must not only be cultivated, but someone has to spin the thread from the boll. The Old and New World looms are remarkably similar in design, and the methods of weaving were strikingly alike in the Eastern and Western Hemispheres. Anyone seeing ancient fabrics from Egypt and Peru will immediately sense a relationship.[133] Completely independent development is untenable because it would infer (1) an unexplained hybridization of Old and New World strains; as well as (2) the idea of spinning thread from the cotton boll; (3) the invention of the same types of looms; and (4) the application of the same weaving techniques for making the fabrics— all simultaneously in distant parts of the world completely out of touch with one another! Moreover the uses of the fabrics in Egypt and Peru include highly specialized applications such as mummy shrouds.

One of the arguments used against diffusion is the absence of certain

Statuette of Egyptian woman tending fire. From Giza, Fifth Dynasty (ca. 2300 B.C.). Grinding flour for baking bread is a feature that is not universal, yet spans the Old and New Worlds. COURTESY, MUSEUM OF FINE ARTS, BOSTON

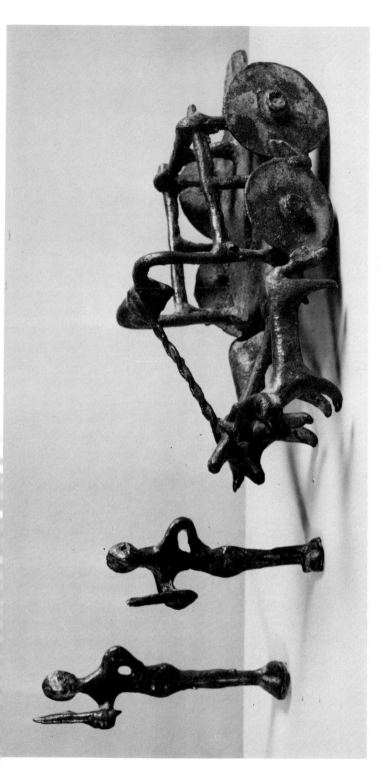

Copper chariot and warriors, from Anatolia, end of third millennium B.C. *Wheeled animal-drawn vehicles in miniature have been found in Mesoamerican excavations, showing Old World influence precisely because draft animals and wheeled vehicles were not used in pre-Columbian America.*

COURTESY, MUSEUM OF FINE ARTS, BOSTON

features in one of the two cultures being compared. For example,
metallurgy did not characterize Mayan civilization down to the fall of
the classical Mayan cities around A.D. 900 when enemies from Mexico
contributed to the general collapse. The martial advantage of the invaders endowed with metal weapons may be compared with the superiority of the Philistines who monopolized metallurgy to the detriment
of the Hebrews whom they kept disarmed.[134]

But throughout their Classical Period (A.D. 300–900), the Mayans
built great stone cities without metal tools. Does this mean that they
had not been exposed to cultures skilled in working gold, silver, copper, bronze or iron? Not at all! People may elect to shun things or
institutions that are well known in their ecumene. Jews and Muslims
avoid pork in a world that domesticates swine for food. To find similar
situations regarding metallurgy in antiquity, we need only know where
to look. The Spartans sensed that precious metals, which go hand in
hand with corruption, ought to be banned in the interest of civic recti-
tude. Accordingly, the Spartan state was disinclined to coin gold and
silver and instead fostered the use of cumbersome iron rings in place
of conventional money. A mina of gold for many individuals is a po-
tent temptation; a mina of iron is far less likely to induce a politician
to sell his soul. In this regard Sparta stood alone among the Greek
cities. Similarly in Egypt we read in the *Contendings of Horus and
Seth* that a ferryman named Anty was derelict in his duty as a result
of accepting a gold signet ring as a bribe. He therefore abjured gold
"unto this day" and declared: "Gold has been made an abomination
for me and for my city." [135]

When Exodus 20:23 prohibits the manufacture of "gods of silver
. . . and gods of gold," it obviously does not imply that such idols
were unknown to the Hebrews. Judges 17:4 tells of an early Hebrew
who commissioned a silversmith to cast an idol out of two hundred
shekels of silver. We also have records outlawing the use of base metal.
Deuteronomy 27:5 represents Moses as instructing the Children of
Israel to build on Mount Ebal, when they will have entered the Prom-
ised Land, an altar of stone without using iron. The latter detail was
of such importance that it is repeated in Joshua 8:31, which states that
when Joshua fulfilled the instructions of Moses, he set up the altar in

Ebal of whole stones without using iron. The Mayans were not less religious than the Hebrews, and both people were capable of intentionally rejecting elements that were common in their ecumene.

Creative people accept and build on certain factors in their environment, while rejecting and even rebelling against other factors. The faith that gave the Mayans the drive to build Tikal [136] could also impose restraints.

Nowhere is the interdependence of the Old and New Worlds clearer than in the domain of science. Astronomy, mathematics and chronology bridge the two worlds so inextricably that it is impossible to understand the history of science in the one without the other. Science is the product of internationalism, not of regionalism. To establish by observations the cycle of eclipses, for example, it is necessary to have global coverage, because the same eclipse need not be visible from the same observation areas in successive cycles.[137] This is one of the reasons that astronomers require observatories in many parts of the world. We know that ancient navigators made celestial observations at the ends of the earth which they reported back to their native regions, for Herodotus (4:42) tells that the Phoenicians claimed that, as they sailed West past the Cape of Good Hope, the sun was on their right. This we now know to be correct because they were in the Southern Hemisphere. Herodotus neither understood nor believed this observation, but like a good reporter passed it on to us. Since the Phoenicians made this celestial observation south of Africa, but transmitted it to the East Mediterranean where scholars like Herodotus could incorporate it into the body of general knowledge, we see how science in the Near East was fed by facts gathered globally. The same holds true for advanced science anywhere, today as well as in the days of Herodotus.

Mathematics went hand in hand with astronomy in laying the foundation for chronology to reckon with days, months, years, cycles and eons. The Mayan year was more precise than any devised by the Old World civilizations; and the Mayans dealt with numbers far greater than European scientists recorded until the Renaissance. Like the civilized people of the ancient Near East and Mediterranean, the Mesoamericans did not separate science and religion. A star, a day of the week or month, a number and a god might all be one. We inherit great segments of this system. Sunday is the day of the Sun; Monday, of the Moon; Tuesday, of Tiw; Wednesday, of Woden; Thursday, of Thor; Friday, of Frigu; and Saturday, of Saturn. Even the Jews, who have so consciously tried to divest themselves of pagan vestiges, call the seventh day *Shabbat,* "Sabbath," though *Shabbatai* is the Hebrew name for Saturn.

The Mesopotamians have left us a detailed record of the interplay of heavenly bodies, gods and numbers. Ishtar is simultaneously a planet (Venus), a goddess and the deified number "15." Her father is Sin: a god, specifically the Moon, and the deified number "30." The god Shamash is the Sun, as well as the deified number "20." The storm god Adad is the deified number "10." Anu, the God of Heaven, is the deified number "1." Also in Egypt, the great god Re, giver of life, is the deified "1." [138]

Greek philosophers, from Pythagoras to Plotinus, have explained the phenomenon of deified numbers. Plotinus gives a full and satisfying essay on why the deified number "1" is the Creator or Prime Mover. [139] "One" is God, because the difference between "0" and "1" is the difference between nonexistence and existence. This cannot be said of the difference between "1" and "2" or between "2" and "3," etc., which are all multiples of "1." When the prophet Zechariah (14:9) declares: "On that day, the Lord shall be 'One' and His name 'One,' " he means exactly what he says: that God is the divine "1." Biblical monotheism should not continue to be understood merely at its most naïve level; namely, that there is a god, and no other god. There is, in addition, a much more profound level of Biblical monotheism which the Hebrews shared with many sophisticated ancient peoples including not only the Greeks, but the civilized inhabitants of Middle America for whom "One" was the Creator. Nor did the Hebrews eliminate the vestiges of other divine numbers. The former name of Hebron was *Qiryat-Arba^c* "City of the [deified number] Four" which we can compare with the Assyrian city *Arba-Ilu* (" 'Four' is God") now called Erbil. Beersheba (*Be'er-Sheba^c*) can only mean "The Well/Cistern of [the deified number] Seven." Bathsheba means "The Daughter of [the deified number] Seven"; and the name of the Judean Princess Jehosheba (Hebrew *Y^eho-sheba^c*) combines God's name Jeho- (short for Yahweh "Jehovah") with the deified number "Seven." This point should be stressed because it illustrates how links between the Old World and ancient America are beginning to clarify even the most intimate and sacred aspects of our own culture.

The preceding point shows that religion, as we know it, was inseparable from the exact sciences of antiquity. Religion among primitive peoples may be called primitive religion, but in the Western tradition, religion is not prescientific but postscientific. We have illustrated this with the monotheistic principle of Scripture. The same holds not only for the calendars that have reached us through Judaism and Christianity, but also for many of our spiritual ideals. Thus the Biblical ideal of international peace when nation shall no longer lift up sword against nation [140] came as a result of international trade which cannot flourish without peace among the nations. And let us not forget that international trade has fostered since remote antiquity the arts of civilization: writing, navigation, manufacturing technologies, etc.

Even the darker sides of culture are intertwined with science and religion. Lucky and unlucky numbers (like 7 and 13 respectively), lucky and unlucky days, and the excesses of astrology are outgrowths of the same concerns that produced mathematics and astronomy. The Babylonians, Greeks, Hebrews and Mesoamericans ascribed great importance to these superstitions as well as to the exact and scientific developments. In a sense this fits into the pattern of what we now call "relevance," for it applies science to ourselves and our actions here and now.[141] Lest we scorn the ancients for their superstitions, let us remember that our newspapers to this day print more astrology than astronomy.

The Maya thought of history in terms of ages, much like Hesiod's ages of man. This kind of thinking is accompanied by eschatology (= the doctrine of the End of Days) such as we find in the Biblical books of Daniel and Revelation. In Judaism it crops up periodically in messianic movements; and in Christianity, in millennial expectations. The Swedish-American colony in Jerusalem was the result of expecting an "end of days" so that groups of Swedes from Sweden and Minnesota sold all their worldly goods and went to Jerusalem, which is the place for believing Jews and Christians to be at "the end of days." Eschatological thinking often posits a cataclysm before the golden age can be ushered in by a messianic figure. The horrible destruction that shall accompany the Battle of Armageddon can terrify a community of believers. The fall of classical Mayan civilization about A.D. 900 has never been fully explained. Often the collapse of a great civilization has internal as well as external causes. We have mentioned an external cause: the onslaught of warlike invaders from Mexico. An internal cause may have been the expectation of an eschatological End of Days that immobilized the Mayans and put a stop to their building and other activities. We have shown that Mesoamericans had messianic expectations, for in A.D. 1519, the Aztecs were expecting the return of the beneficent white god, Quetzalcoatl, and this played into the hands of Cortés and his band of Spanish conquistadores who by sheer coincidence arrived that year.

Early Spanish observers of Indian life in Mesoamerica noticed institutions that suggested Near Eastern, and specifically Biblical, origins. For instance, the Aztecs punished adultery with stoning to death.[142] Since this is prescribed in Scripture, it was interpreted as indicating that the Indians were the Lost Tribes of Israel. Now that we have a broader concept of the Bible World, we need not confuse the Aztec institution with any myth of the Lost Tribes. The specific punishment for a specific offense may have been a law that the Hebrews and Aztecs inherited ultimately from a common source.[143] Similarly the Cross of the pre-Columbian Indians, need not indicate, as many a Spanish priest fancied, Christian influence. The Cross is widespread as a sacred symbol. Indeed the Christian Cross embodies certain Egyptian elements, notably the looped cross standing for *ankh* "life."

Human sacrifice, whereby great numbers of captives are grimly offered up to a god, characterized both Canaanite and Aztec religions. The Moabite King Mesha tells us on his stela how he sacrificed thousands of captives to his god Chemosh.[144] Even the Hebrews practiced this grim rite at Jericho [145] and Ai [146] in the days of Joshua; nor was it considered wrong by the prophet Samuel in the days of King Saul.[147] We find the sacrifice of captives among the Maya, but nowhere was it practiced to such excesses as among the Aztecs.

Trade in Middle America enjoyed special status. It was sponsored by the ruler and held in honor. All this smacks of Old World institutions especially in the Near East, culminating in the Phoenicians whose lords were merchant princes. Among the Aztecs no commercial mission was set in motion without at least one human heart offered to some god.[148]

It is interesting to note that the Canaanite inscription from Brazil mentions the sacrifice of a youth when the expedition was launched. Moreover, that text, which singles out a Phoenician sovereign as the "merchant king" who sponsored the mission, constitutes a specific link connecting a great Old World commercial center with ancient America.

Chapter IX

THE POPOL VUH
AND THE ANCIENT
NEAR EAST

ONE OF THE DIFFICULTIES in comparing Old and New World civilizations is the uneven distribution of extant and intelligible written sources. Classical Europe, the Near East, India and China have left abundant written literatures, whereas there is relatively little from pre-Columbian America, and the Mayan texts that have survived are largely undeciphered except for the date formulae. Part of the problem is a consequence of an unfortunate aspect of Spanish history during the Conquest. Spain was suffering from the anti-intellectualism built into the book-burning mentality of the Inquisition so that only three of the Mayan codices have survived: one in Dresden, another in Madrid, the third in Paris. To be sure, not all the Spanish priests were book burners, and some devoted their lives to salvaging whatever information they could of the great cultures in New Spain.

By far the most important American Indian text is the *Popol Vuh: The Sacred Book of the Ancient Quiché Maya* (English version by Delia Goetz and Sylvanus G. Morley, University of Oklahoma Press, Norman, 1950), which we shall abbreviate "P.V." Around A.D. 1550, an anonymous but educated member of the Quiché Maya (= the Maya of the Guatemalan highlands) reedited the sacred text in the native language transcribed in Latin letters. The text presents the cosmological concepts, ancient traditions and the history of their origins with the generations of their kings from the Creation to about

A.D. 1550 when the text was reconstituted and brought up to date. Toward the close of the seventeenth century, Father Francisco Ximénez, who was then parish priest in Santo Tomás Chichicastenango, borrowed and copied the now-lost sixteenth-century manuscript of P.V. from one of his parishioners. Ximénez, who knew the native language, was the first to translate the P.V. into Spanish. Before the Conquest, the P.V. in native script was treasured as scripture, as is clear from a passage in the sixteenth-century manuscript which Ximénez translates: "And there was a place where they could see everything, and a book of all, which they call Book of the Community [i.e., Popol Vuh]" (P.V., p. 225, n. 3). The Maya therefore had canonical Scripture which, like the Bible, was regarded as revealing everything worth preserving and knowing about the universe, past history and the future.

The Quiché describe their ancestors as "coming from the other side of the sea" (P.V., pp. 79–80). Those original ancestors, who were products of the last of several creations, were four in number and bore the names: Balam-Quitzé, Balam-Acab, Mahucutah and Iqui-Balam. That they arrived across the Atlantic, and not the Pacific, is clear from the statement that they came to what is now the Guatemalan highlands "from the other side of the sea, where the sun rises" (P.V., p. 206). This tradition is confirmed by the Aztec insistence that Quetzalcoatl, who came to Mexico across the Atlantic from the east, introduced "all the mechanical arts, such as the smelting of silver, stone- and wood-carving, painting, making feather-work, and other trades" (Bernardino de Sahagun, *A History of Ancient Mexico,* translated by Fanny R. Bandelier, Vol. I, Fisk University Press, Nashville, Tennessee, 1932, p. 188).

The P.V. indicates that contact was for a while maintained between Maya land and the mother country across the sea. The Maya of P.V. were divided into three groups (Cavec, Nihaib, and Ahau-Quiché), each tracing its descent from one of the Four Ancestors. Qocaib, the son of Balam-Quitzé, of the Cavec; Qoacutes, son of Balam-Acab, of the Nihaib; and Qoahau, son of Mahucutah, of the Ahau-Quiché, decided to go "to the East, there whence came our fathers" and proceeded "to the other side of the sea" in "the East"— "to receive the investiture of the kingdom." "The Lord, King of the

East . . . Lord Nacxit . . . supreme judge of all the kingdoms . . . gave them the insignia of the kingdom and all its distinctive symbols" (P.V., p. 207). The canonical tradition thus implies that of old the Maya recognized the suzerainty of the Old World homeland, from which it received its authority and symbols, which can hardly be divorced from the American hieroglyphs. Qocaib, Qoacutes and Qoahau then returned to the Maya highlands to rule over their tribes (P.V., p. 209).

P.V. reflects, at different levels, many cultural tie-ins with the Old World. For example the Maya warriors included "bowmen and slingers" (P.V., p. 222). The sling and particularly the bow and arrow are not simple inventions like the knife or pounding stone, but are complex. Both bowmen and slingers are singled out in the texts of the ancient Greeks, Hebrews and other Old World people as regular branches of the military. The Old World contexts, like P.V., has to do with the technology of warfare.

In our study, it is just as important to note the character of flights of fancy as it is to compare the accomplishments of the down-to-earth engineers. The tribes "crossed the sea, the waters having parted when they passed" (P.V., p. 183). This of course is the same miracle described in Exodus (14:21-23; 15:8, 9) when the waters of the Red Sea parted so that the Children of Israel crossed on dry land.

P.V., p. 96, records a myth about two deities long ago: Vucub-Caquix tore off the arm of Hun-Hunahpú, which may hark back to the origin of the Egyptian portrayal of the god Min, who has only one arm.

Two beloved gods, destined for resurrection—Hunahpú and Xba-lanqué—were put to death "in a bonfire," after which their bones were crushed "on a grinding stone, as corn meal is ground" (pp. 154–155). In Ugaritic mythology, the "beloved of the gods," Mot, was put to death by a series of acts including "burning in fire" and "grinding in the millstones" before he was resurrected like Hunahpú and Xba-lanqué. All this goes with fertility rites of a gruesome nature.

There is another striking parallel between P.V. and Ugaritic mythology. Hunahpú and Xbalanqué "felled birds" . . . "built a fire and put the birds in it to roast, but they rubbed one of the birds with chalk (or natural lime cement), covering it with a white earth

A handsome seat of the Akkad period in Mesopotamia (ca. 2300 B.C.). The portrayal of the animals is quite lively. The invention of the bow and arrow can hardly be independent in the Eastern and Western Hemispheres, for the idea and process are complex. COURTESY, MUSEUM OF FINE ARTS, BOSTON

soil" (p. 105) and they then, with intent to kill, gave that bird to Cabracan, who ate it and died. In Ugaritic text #52, the god El felled birds and streaked one or more of them before putting them on the fire to roast. The verb ḫrṭ in this text means "to incise, streak," but until the P.V. parallel was brought to bear, its plain sense was missed, and it was conjecturally translated "to pluck and/or clean (a bird)." It is worth noting that while some scholars incline to explaining such parallels through diffusion, and others through independent development, all are agreed that there are many remarkable similarities among the mythologies of the world so that myths of different peoples illuminate each other's meaning. What is noteworthy here is that New World sources are beginning to shed light on those of the Old World; and not only on esoteric literatures like the Ugaritic, but, as we shall soon note, on the most familiar documents in our tradition, including the opening chapters of Genesis.

The mating of gods with women is quite widespread. In Homeric epic it is routine. And although our officially purified theology tends to shut our eyes to it, the Bible reflects it too. Genesis 6:2–4 states quite plainly that long ago the deities mated with the fair daughters of men to sire the ancient heroes. The most important example in history is also Biblical, for Mary conceived Jesus from the Holy Spirit. The P.V., pp. 119–126, relates that a girl named Xquic, impregnated by divine juice, gave birth to the twin gods Hunahpú and Xbalanqué, who "were really gods" (p. 94). The birth of a pair of gods (Shaḥar "Dawn" and Shalem "Dusk") by womankind impregnated by the great god El is incorporated into Ugaritic text #52.

One of the most striking parallels between P.V. and Old World cosmology has to do with the notion that toothache is caused by a worm. The evil god Vucub-Caquix has a toothache to be cured by removing the worm (P.V., p. 98). It happens that the Babylonians, like the Maya, not only believed that the worm caused toothache, but they attribute it to cosmic origins. When the gods had established the universe, the worm came weeping before the sun god Shamash and the beneficent water god Ea, begging that a source of food be allocated to it. The worm was offered ripe figs and apricots which he scorned, and insisted instead on living among our teeth and gums to suck our blood, which is what plagues us with toothache. The Babylonian magician after reciting this myth invokes the curse of Ea against the worm (J. B. Pritchard, *Ancient Near Eastern Texts*, pp. 100–101).

Another Old World parallel carries us beyond the Near East to India. The Maya, like the Hindus, attributed a different color to each of the four directions. The P.V., pp. 114–115, refers to a "crossroad" where "one of the four roads was red, another black, another white, and another yellow."

Before Creation "there was only immobility and silence in the darkness, in the night. Only the Creator, the Maker, Tepeu, Gucumatz, the Forefathers were in the water surrounded by light" (P.V., p. 81). Thus darkness existed prior to Creation, as in Genesis 1:1–2, which means: "When God set about creating Heaven and Earth, the Earth was chaotic, with darkness over the surface of the Deep, and the Spirit of God flying over the surface of the water." Moreover, water is preexistent in both P.V. and Genesis. Both accounts also associate the Creator(s) with light (but not with darkness). In Genesis the first act of the Creator is " 'Let there be light!' And light came into being" (1:3). Note that the creation in Genesis 1 is by fiat; God utters the creative word, which is immediately translated into fact. P.V., p. 83, deals with the same idea. " 'Earth!' they (the Creators) said, and instantly it was made."

After the Creators brought animals into existence, they realized they would have to create men because the animals "could not understand each other's speech." However, the Creators' first attempt to make man was a failure; he had no durability and even lacked the energy to move. They resolved to try again in order to make men who are capable of locomotion and reproduction. Accordingly "they broke up and destroyed their work and their creation" before making a second attempt (P.V., p. 86).

This brings up an interesting point in the Bible. The first account of man's creation occurs in Genesis 1. On the sixth day, God creates the animal kingdom, climaxing it with man, male and female, as replicas of the gods. God says to the other deities: "Let us make man in our image, as our likeness, so that they [i.e., mankind] may rule over the fish of the sea, over the fowl of the heavens, and over the cattle, and all [the beasts of] the earth, and over all creeping things

that crawl over the earth" (1:26). Then God proceeded to "create
Man in His image—in the image of god(s) he created him—male
and female he created them" (1:27). God then commands mankind
to "be fruitful and multiply and fill the earth, and conquer it and
rule" over the entire animal kingdom, and use the vegetable kingdom
as food (1:28–30). Nothing is said about man's ability to fulfil God's
instructions. He is simply a magnificent effigy in the likeness of the
gods. There is no indication that he could speak, govern, breed or
even walk.

In what we are about to say, no liberty will be taken with the Biblical text. We shall examine it as it is. Obviously, as Judaism and Christianity became more refined, believers have found it harder and harder
to take these ancient pre-Hebraic myths in their stride. And yet, common sense as well as rational method should tell us that we are closer
to the original meaning of the text, if we take it on its own terms, than
we are likely to be by subjecting it to an artificial and alien literary
analysis. In Genesis 1–3 there are two entirely different creation accounts of man. The modern theological notion that God is so perfect
that He cannot make mistakes is not borne out by the Old Testament.
Not only does man disobey Him, but Genesis 6:6–7 plainly states:
"Yahweh regretted that He had made man on the earth, and felt heart-
sick. Yahweh said: 'I shall wipe out the mankind that I have created,
from the face of the earth; yea, from man to beast, to creeping things,
and to the fowl of the heavens; for I regret that I made them.' " God
in the Old Testament is not a perfect machine; He not only makes mistakes, but He regrets them.

Now this brings us to Genesis 2:1–2 after the six days of the First
Creation: "The heavens and the earth and all their host were finished
and God on the seventh day finished His work which He had done."
The Hebrew verb "to finish" (the *piel* conjugation of the root *kly*) can
mean "to complete," but it commonly means "to destroy." Since "to
finish" in English shares this range of meanings, it is the correct translation. The ambiguity of "to finish" may well be intentional. The Semites love plays on words, and a scene in the Gilgamesh Epic hinges on
such a double entendre; for in tablet 11:48, 87, 90, the Flood Hero
deceives the public by telling them that the god Ea will bring "a rain
of wheat" which can also mean "a rain of blight" (i.e., the Flood which

is about to destroy them). An ordinary person is not quick to perceive such nuances, but the enlightened man grasps them. The Gnostics have since antiquity insisted that esoteric knowledge is essential for understanding serious matters, starting with the accounts of Creation. It is possible that the author(s) of Genesis 1–3 wanted to leave the interpretation ambiguous, so that simple people could take a meaning suitable for their level, while the subtle or initiated reader could go deeper. In any case what follows is clear and unambiguous.

A new creation account opens in Genesis 2:4 with the title: "These are the generations [= history] of the heavens and the earth when they were created." The text goes on to tell us there was no vegetation, nor rain, nor any man to till the soil. This time Yahweh-Elohim does not create any beautiful statue, but "fashioned the man with dust from the earth, and blew into his nostrils the breath of life, so that man became a living soul" (2:7). Unlike the first creation of man, this time he is to have real life, with a soul and the ability (as the sequel shows) to walk, speak, work, and (after the creation of woman) to procreate. It is interesting to note that an ancient tradition, preserved in the authoritative Aramaic translation of the Old Testament, interpreted the breath infused into Adam as the ability to speak. God in Genesis, like the Creators in P.V., were not satisfied with a mankind, dumb like the animals. To fulfil his role, man had to have human qualities such as speech.

The Second Creation in the P.V. also left something to be desired. The Creators made men of wood this time (P.V., p. 88). "They looked like men, talked like men, and populated the surface of the earth . . . but they did not have souls, nor minds. . . . These were the first men who existed in great numbers on the face of the earth" (P.V., p. 89). However, their lack of spirit and intelligence kept them from being worthy of serving the gods so that these "wooden figures were annihilated" and "a flood was brought about by the Heart of Heaven . . . on the heads of the wooden creatures" (P.V. p. 90). As in the Bible, a remnant survived the Deluge, but in a very different way. The Maya had a tradition that the monkeys are descended from those wooden figures (P.V., pp. 92–93). They look like men, but are subhuman (unlike Noah who was worthy of perpetuating mankind in the service of God).

One of the details in the Mayan cosmogony has a curious Near East parallel. Hun-Hunahpú, with his two sons Hunbatz and Hunchouén, and with his brother Vucub-Hunahpú, disturbed the Lords of Xibalba by "making so much noise" that the Lords wanted to destroy them (p. 109). In the Babylonian creation epic (1:21–50), Apsu wanted to wipe out the young gods because they made so much noise that he could not rest. In Genesis 18:20–21 it is the noise or outcry in Sodom and Gomorrah that impels Yahweh to destroy those cities. It is interesting to note that the Maya are a very quiet people. Anyone visiting Chichicastenango during the busy market days (Thursdays and Sundays) cannot help observing the quiet that pervades the atmosphere despite the large crowds moving about and transacting business.

The final creation of man followed the divine decision "to make man, and when what must enter into the flesh of man was sought" (P.V., p. 165). The moment was "just before the sun, the moon and the stars appeared over the Creators and Makers" (i.e., Tepeu and Gucumatz; P.V., p. 165). Describing the state of the heavenly bodies to provide the timing of mythological events reflects the society in which no serious step was taken without consulting the astrologers who knew when celestial beings appeared auspiciously in the sky. Thus Ugaritic text #77, times the birth of a wondrous child by the moon-goddess "when the Sun sets [and] the Moon *rises*(?)." Job 38:4–7 states that God laid the foundations of the earth "when the stars of morning sang together and all of the deities shouted" in joyous song. Like the P.V., the Bible thus describes the heavenly host at the time of creation.

This time the Creators made sure that man would not be wooden or soulless and insisted: "Let those who are to nourish and sustain us appear, the noble sons, the civilized vassals; let man appear, humanity on the face of the earth" (P.V., p. 165). The Bible similarly describes the new creation of man by Yahweh-Elohim who makes sure that this time He will not be stuck with a soulless statue unable to do His bidding. He fashioned the man and breathed into his nostrils a breath of life so that the man became a living soul (Genesis 2:7). The gods in the Bible as well as P.V. learned from trial and error as they created us in stages. In neither tradition, did they achieve perfection.

P.V., p. 168, notes that the newly created men were this time "endowed with intelligence; they saw and instantly they could see far, they succeeded in seeing, they succeeded in knowing all that there is in the world." Those men could boast: "We also see the large and the small in the sky and on earth." In other words, "they were able to know all" (P.V., p. 169). This indeed is what happened to the mankind created anew and infused with living souls. Adam and Eve obtained universal knowledge "knowing good and evil" (Genesis 3:5) so that "the eyes of both of them were opened" (3:7). Much ink has been spilled over the pair of antonyms "good and evil." Such antonymic pairs simply express totality, and can often be translated as "everything." Not only "good and evil" but also "large and small" are among such pairs used in the Bible and other literatures. Thus the P.V. and Genesis describe mankind as "knowing everything"; and both traditions tell us in no uncertain terms that the gods did not like the fact that their creatures rivaled them in possessing the divine attribute of universal knowledge. P.V., p. 169, puts it this way: "But the Creator and the Maker did not hear this with pleasure. 'It is not well what our creatures, our works say; they know all, the large and the small. . . . What shall we do with them now? . . . Must they also be gods? . . . Must they perchance be the equals of ourselves, their Makers, who can see afar, who know all and see all?' . . . Then the Heart of Heaven blew mist into their eyes, which clouded their sight . . . and they could see only what was close. . . . In this way the wisdom and all the knowledge of the four [created] men . . . were destroyed."

There are differences between the P.V. and Genesis creations; e.g., P.V. has the creators making four men, whereas Genesis limits it to a single man. But the concepts inherent in the two versions are unmistakably akin. Yahweh-Elohim, like the P.V. Creators, declares to the other deities: "Since man has become like one of us, knowing good and evil [= everything], what is to stop him from stretching forth his hand and taking also [fruit] from the Tree of Life, eating it and living forever" (Genesis 3:22)? There is no mistaking the meaning of the text, for in Genesis 3:5 the Serpent has already predicted: "For God knows that on the day you eat thereof [i.e., the fruit of the Tree of Knowledge] your eyes will be opened and you will be like gods, knowing good and evil [= everything]." The gods want us to be intelligent enough to serve them properly, but they do not want us to become their equals, and the P.V. and Bible inform us that as soon as the gods realized the danger, they trimmed us down to size.

The P.V. and the Bible also agree that man came first, and that woman was fashioned later while man slept. "Then their wives had being, and their women were made. God himself made them carefully. And so, during sleep, they came, truly beautiful . . . at the side of [the four created men:] Balam-Quitzé, Balam-Acab, Mahucutah and Iqui-Balam" (P.V., p. 170). Genesis 2:21–22 relates that "Yahweh-Elohim caused a sleep to descend on the man, so that he slept. And He took one of his ribs and covered it with flesh. And God fashioned the rib which He took from the man into a woman, and he brought her to the man."

It may be a mere coincidence, but it is curious that P.V. traces the human race to four men and four women, even as the Bible derives all surviving humanity from Noah and his three sons and four women: one wife for each of the four men saved on the Ark.

The preludes to human procreation in P.V. and Genesis have much in common. In both cases, the process is heralded by a woman who takes wondrous fruit from a special tree, though she feared it might mean death. P.V., p. 119, tells of a maiden who, in days of yore, heard of the fruit and mused: "Surely the fruit of which I hear tell must be very good. . . . What fruit is this which this tree bears? . . . Must I die, shall I be lost, if I pick one of this fruit?" A piece of the fruit that happened also to be the skull of the god Hun-Hunahpú told the girl to reach for the fruit. When she did so, some spittle from the skull dropped on her palm so that she conceived the twin gods Hunahpú and Xbalanqué (P.V., p. 120). In the Biblical account, Eve tells the Serpent that it is permitted to eat the fruit of any tree in the Garden except one concerning which God said: "Do not eat thereof, and do not touch it, lest you die" (Genesis 3:3). But the Serpent, like Hun-Hunahpú, tells her to go ahead and eat it. She does so, and also gives some to Adam, with the result that they become aware of their nakedness [i.e., sex], and the knowledge from that Tree of Knowledge started the procreation of humanity: "For the man knew Eve his wife, and she conceived and bore Cain" (Genesis 4:1).

Both the P.V. and the Bible state the same apparent contradiction:

that after man multiplied on the earth and the groups of men were speaking different languages, all men nonetheless spoke one language. This can only mean that in addition to the various "languages of the world," there was a universal "lingua franca" that all men understood and used for intergroup communication. P.V., p. 172, states: "There they were then, in great number, the black men and the white men, men of many classes, men of many tongues, that it was wonderful to hear them" and yet the text goes on to say "The speech of all was the same."

In the same fashion, Genesis 10:5, 20, 30 explicitly states that mankind multiplied after the flood and split up into different groups, speaking various languages. But the very first verse of Genesis 11 notes that the entire world had "one language" with a fixed vocabulary. In any ecumene of intercommunicating nations speaking different languages, there must be a lingua franca. Long ago in the West, it was Latin; more recently, French; now, English is becoming *de facto* the lingua franca globally.

The fact that both the P.V. and Genesis 10–11 state the multiplicity of language alongside the existence of a single language for all mankind shows that it is futile to reckon with each tradition in a vacuum, or to assume that the Maya and the Hebrews were too stupid to detect a contradiction within the span of a few verses. We have explained how the contradiction is apparent, not real.

The breakup of the "one language," leading to the disunity and scattering of mankind, is also shared by P.V. and the Bible. The P.V. (p. 176) version runs: "the speech of the tribes changed: their tongues became different. They could no longer understand each other clearly after arriving at Tulan. There also they separated, there were some who had to go to the East [Yucatán], but many came here." Genesis 11:1-9 relates, in the story of the Tower of Babel, that mankind with "one language" was cooperating in building a city with a tower that would reach heaven, and thus (for reasons that are not yet clear) they would make "a name" for themselves and not be scattered over the face of the earth. But their aim was unacceptable to Yahweh, who confounded the "one language" so that they could no longer understand one another and were forced to abandon the work. Yahweh proceeded to scatter them throughout the earth.

The Mayan preoccupation with numbers is comparable not only in degree but also in kind with numerology in certain areas of ancient Near East culture. Mesopotamian mathematics comes to mind, starting in the Bronze Age. The Pythagoreans absorbed and developed the system, making it a part of Greek science and philosophy. We can only point out a few specific numbers singled out for emphasis in both the Old and New Worlds. P.V. (pp. 99–101, 163–164) tells of the four hundred youths who became the four hundred stars of the sky to accompany Hunahpú and Xbalanqué that became the Sun and the Moon. Thus "four hundred" is a conventional numeral to indicate "a great host" or "large number of." It is applied frequently in the Old Testament to people, animals, years, quantities of metal, etc. It refers to groups of people (as in the P.V. passages just cited) in Genesis 33:1; Judges 20:2, 17; 21:12; 1 Samuel 30:17; 1 Kings 18:19; 2 Chronicles 18:5; and so forth.

The stress on "seven" is widespread—and we are only scratching the surface in pointing out the following few examples. P.V. (pp. 136, 137, 139) mentions "within seven days" recalling the seven-day week that starts in the Western tradition with Genesis 1. The obsession with "seven" is reflected by the Hebrew system of heptads; seven days make a week; seven weeks mark the span of time from Passover to Pentacost; the Jewish New Year is in the seventh (not the first!) month; seven years make a sabbatical cycle; seven sabbatical cycles make a Jubilee. The numeral "7" (*sheba^c* in Hebrew) is deified in the names *Eli-sheba^c* "Elizabeth" and *Yeho-sheba^c* "Jehosheba." This preoccupation with "seven" also pervades the records and institutions of Mesopotamia, Egypt, Ugarit, Greece, etc. A good Mayan example is P.V., pp. 219–220: "for seven days he [Gucumatz] mounted to the skies and for seven days he went down to Xibalba; seven days he changed himself into a snake and really became a serpent; for seven days he changed himself into an eagle; for seven days he became a jaguar; and his appearance was really that of an eagle and a jaguar. Another seven days he changed himself into clotted blood and was only motionless blood." Doubling numbers is also found among the Maya and ancient Near Easterners. Specifically "fourteen" or "twice seven" in P.V., pp. 140–142, is found in Mesopotamia, Canaan, Greece and elsewhere.

The P.V., pp. 204–205, has the "Four Patriarchs" (Balam-Quitzé, Balam-Acab, Mahucutah and Iqui-Balam), in anticipation of their death, giving orally their last wills and testaments to their children. They then give names to the children, and prophesy to them: "Go on your way and you shall see again the place from which we came." In the Jewish tradition "The Testaments of the Twelve Patriarchs" is the fullest development of this theme, but it is already an integral part of the patriarchal narratives of Genesis, in which the aged Isaac, anticipating death, "blesses" his sons Jacob and Esau and predicts their future roles (Genesis 27). A fuller development is attested in Genesis 49 where the aged patriarch Jacob summons his sons to predict what will happen to them in the future (v. 1), calling each of them by name (verses 3–27) and in a number of cases singling out their animal affinities (Judah is a lion; Issachar, an ass; Naphtali, a gazelle; and Benjamin, a wolf). As in P.V., so too in the Bible, starting with Genesis (15:7–16), the descendants of the patriarchs are destined to wander from the ancestral land, but will eventually return to it. The return to the ancestral land is a major theme in the Bible (New as well as Old Testament), and it spread to Rome (for it is enshrined in the national epic: Vergil's Aeneid) apparently from the Jews (C. H. Gordon, "Vergil and the Near East," pp. 277–278).

The P.V. (p. 171), like the Bible, divides the people into three groups—note Genesis 10 which views all mankind as descendants of the three brothers Shem, Ham and Japheth. The P.V. (p. 175) states that the three Quiché families were held together not only by the oneness of their god but of that god's name (i.e., Tohil). The Hebrew account of the unification of the tribes goes hand in hand with the emphasis on the One God worshiped by his name Yahweh. Joshua (24:14–15) tells all the assembled tribes of Israel (v. 1) that they have to decide on what god they want to worship, but "I and my house will serve Yahweh" (v. 15). The foundations of unity are laid when the tribes unanimously accept Yahweh as their god: "Far be it from us to forsake Yahweh and serve other gods" (v. 16).

P.V., pp. 214–215, tells how the three clans (the Cavec, Nihaib and Ahau-Quiché) united, abandoning the town of Izmachi and centering on the town of Gumarcaah, thus paralleling the Biblical narrative of the tribes of Israel centering around a series of cultic shrines, such as Shiloh and later Jerusalem. "There had then begun the fifth generation of men, since the beginning of civilization and of the population, the beginning of the existence of the nation." The Bible too carefully records the generations from Adam and Eve, through Noah to the establishment of the people in the person of Abraham, and then the genealogies are continued without interruption into the New Testament (Matthew 1).

P.V., p. 217, goes on to record that as the Mayan "empire grew" there arose division, jealousy and dissension; paralleling the Biblical tale of the internecine warfare of the tribes, and the splitting of the united monarchy founded by David and enhanced by Solomon into the two kingdoms of northern Israel and southern Judah.

P.V. (pp. 220, 229–230) is concerned not only with the genealogies of civilized man (i.e., the Maya) from the creation, but specifically with the genealogy of the Mayan kings from the creation to the time when the text was written. This holds for the Chronicles of the Kings of Judah, and of the Chronicles of the Kings of Israel, which were used (and cited by name) in compiling the Biblical Books of Kings; and for the Biblical Books of Chronicles and the New Testament. Luke 3:23–38 traces the genealogy of Christ, who is King of the Jews, back through David and Abraham to Adam; Matthew 1 traces it back through David to Abraham, who was not only the first Hebrew but also the founder of the royal line. The Jews perpetuated the tradition of the royal Davidic line into Roman times, calling the heirs to the throne *Nasi,* an old word for "king" or "prince" but *de facto* "the ethnarch" respected by the people, but powerless vis-à-vis the alien government. (For Abraham as the founder of the royal line, see Genesis 17:6.)

The twelfth generation of kings was hanged by the Spanish under the Adelantado Don Pedro de Alvarado, who conquered Central America. The thirteenth generation of kings, Tecum and Tepepul, paid tribute to the Spaniards. The fourteenth generation of kings were the sons of Tecum and Tepepul, and bore the names Don Juan de Rojas and Don Juan Cortes. The P.V., which was compiled about A.D. 1550, gives the subdivisions of the three Quiché tribes, much as the Old Testament delineates the subdivision of the twelve tribes into clans.

P.V., pp. 234–235, ends on the hopeless note that "all the people of the Quiché" has come "to an end." The Bible, on this point, is entirely different, for it conveys a message of hope and the conviction that God's plan for His people cannot be thwarted by catastrophe, for in the End of Days history must give way to the Golden Age that will endure for eternity.

Chapter X

SUMMATION

THE MESOAMERICANS have a consistent tradition that civilization was brought to their shores by a bearded white being who came from the east by boat. This echoes the cultural impact of Western Europe and the Mediterranean—mainly the latter, which endured as an influential cradle of civilization since Neolithic times. By the Middle Bronze Age, the Mediterranean under its Minoan thalassocrats possessed a transoceanic communications capability.

The trend of archeological discovery is to confirm the traditions against the hyperskeptical denial fostered by overspecialization. Before Schliemann uncovered Troy—and Evans, Knossos—the consensus of learned opinion regarded the Homeric traditions as myth. Now we can study the history and read the texts of the Minoans and Mycenaeans. This book implies that the legends of Quetzalcoatl, like the Greek legends, reflect historic movements.

We have many Greek and some Hebrew sources referring to contacts with America. The tenth chapter of Genesis includes in the ecumene, not only the Near East heartland, but also remote "islands" [149] discovered and developed by enterprising merchant mariners from that heartland. The South Arabians are credited with colonizing far-off Ophir,[150] rich in gold; the Greeks, with colonizing Tarshish [151] in the farthest West, famed for its silver. We have seen how not only native traditions, but also the place-names and the Indian languages of America provide us with material for reconstructing the history of the Western Hemisphere within its global setting.

The most vivid evidence for the nature of the populations of Mesoamerica is the host of sculptured heads of stone, and especially of terracotta. Far Eastern types, including the Chinese and Japanese, African Negroes, and various Caucasians including Semites, are portrayed unmistakably in the art of pre-Columbian Middle America. Indeed the living Indian types (such as the Mayans and Aztecs) first appear around the dawn of the Classical Period about A.D. 300. Before then, we find various Old World types of people in Mesoamerica. Accordingly there is at our disposal a "picture album" of the people who brought the ingredients of classical civilization to the shores of Middle America. Some types are clear enough for present purposes; e.g., Chinese in pigtails, blacks with flat noses and thick lips, or the Mediterranean merchant prince from Iximché. Refinements will gradually be made by specialists qualified to determine what branch of the Chinese what tribe of Negroes, and what ethnic group of the Mediterranean each of those figurines specifically portrays. Moreover, less familiar and problematic types occur such as Ainu-like faces whose investigation may open new vistas of world history. A myriad of details confront us. Many can be understood and put in perspective; many more will require long and patient study. But we can already discern broad outlines that are emerging with clarity.

Thales of Miletus according to Herodotus (1:74) in 585 B.C. predicted an eclipse (which actually occurred on May 28 of that year). Saint Augustine (*City of God* 8:2) states that Thales was able to predict solar and lunar eclipses through his knowledge of astronomical calculations. If scientists, by Augustine's time, established the cycle of eclipses through observation, they must have done so on the basis of global coverage. More precisely, the minimal coverage required for establishing the cycle is at three longitudinal bands, 120° apart. If we regard the Near East as the center of ancient science, 120° to the west takes us to Middle America: another area of scientific observation and development. If we travel 120° east of the Near East center, we are in the western Pacific. In the south, the longitudinal line runs through the Solomon Islands (whose native populations include a white strain) and in the north through the northern islands of Japan where the white

Ainu remnant lingers on. Can these natives be the survivors of ancients who spread and developed culture around the Pacific? China, of course, is the great land of ancient science [152] in the West Pacific, and, for reasons that we have pointed out (and another about to be stated below), China must have played a significant role in linking the Old World with ancient America.

While schematizations are always somewhat contrived, they may be useful in helping us organize our thoughts. It is therefore suggested that we visualize the founders of ancient astronomy as setting up bases in the Near East, Middle America and the West Pacific for the observations they needed to establish their science. Next let us visualize the ancients as filtering their observations into a "center" for processing, like the Phoenicians who made a celestial observation while rounding the Cape of Good Hope, and then transmitted it to the Mediterranean center.

Vast geographical and chronological spreads must be taken into consideration, but we ought to beware of being stunned by them into mental inertia. First, we must understand that various seafaring people of antiquity mastered the arts of shipbuilding and navigation sufficiently for crossing oceans. Next we have to realize that human habits and memory can persist for millennia. Methods of agriculture, weaving or preparing bread have endured virtually unchanged among peasants of Mesoamerica and the Orient for thousands of years. The Jews have not forgotten that Nebuchadnezzar of Babylon destroyed their Temple in 586 B.C. Illiterate Mayan peasants in Guatemala preserve aspects of their ancient ancestors' skill at calendrical calculation, which they still perform with amazing speed. Syro-Palestinian Arab peasants still call rain-fed land, *ba'l*, but land that must be irrigated to be productive, *mawāt*. This terminology is rooted in Canaanite antiquity, when Ba'l was worshiped as the god of fertility and Mawt as the god of sterility. Two millennia of Christianity and Islam have not obliterated the vestiges of an ancient pagan past. For this reason, a hypercritical denial of relationships between cultural phenomena attested in different periods can be just as misleading as the naïve equation of superficially similar phenomena.

Charles H. Hapgood has noted that a number of early maps incorporate factual elements of ancient cartography that could not have been based on the defective knowledge current at the time when our copies of the maps were made. For example, the Piri Reis map of 1513 shows the correct longitudinal relationship between the east coast of South America and the west coast of Africa. Modern science had devised no satisfactory way of determining longitude until the eighteenth century when the chronometer was invented. Therefore the Piri Reis map (which, as Piri Reis himself states in writing, incorporates material from ancient maps in the Library at Alexandria) reflects a lost ancient science when men were able to determine longitude through other means (presumably lunar observations). A twelfth-century map of China similarly has features that link it to *the same* science in remote antiquity.[153] The maps scrutinized by Hapgood even include the essentially correct delineation of the Antarctic coastline that has been under ice for at least six thousand years. Accordingly, there was an age when men crossed oceans and developed a scientific school of cartography long before we have any evidence of writing. Hapgood's pioneering work must be used critically; but after all its shortcomings are exposed by the merciless critics, the fact remains that it is one of the great books of our time. He concludes (p. 145) that there was in very ancient times a worldwide civilization whose cartographers mapped virtually the entire globe with a uniform level of mathematics and technology, and by similar methods.

A completely different approach is provided by Moran and Kelley, who have shown that ancient mariners, skilled in celestial navigation, used lunar zodiac signs for keeping track of the days in the month. Moreover, our alphabet is derived from a set of such signs. Since interrelated lunar zodiacs are found in pre-Columbian America as well as in various parts of the Old World, the network of mariners who fostered the system spanned the Old and New Worlds. They should not be considered as a people tied to a particular land; they were a Sea People, perhaps made of several ethnic and linguistic elements. They played a key role in the history of world civilization, including the devising of our alphabet.[154] They are unquestionably associated with the Minoans and Phoenicians, however much the details remain to be worked out. Quite independently, Moran and Kelley have arrived at

the same general conclusions as Hapgood: that there was a scientifically and technologically developed civilization that penetrated virtually every part of the world in remote antiquity.

Hebrew, Greek, Mesopotamian, Egyptian and other literatures of
antiquity refer to a golden age in the distant past. Actually if we look
at the monuments of bygone ages, we note something striking. The
most impressive monuments of Egypt are the great pyramids going
back to the Early Bronze Age. The most monumental structures of
Malta and pre-Roman Britain are megalithic temples of the Bronze
Age. Such achievements can not be the work of primitive men starting
from scratch with nothing but independent invention to raise them
from barbarism. Their structures are masterpieces of architecture and
engineering that reflect long scientific and technological development.
Moreover, the technical interrelations among early builders in various
parts of the world point to some common background, rooted in a
great, earlier culture on which they all drew.[155]

The links we have observed between the Old World and America
reflect the contributions of numerous peoples, from different directions, during many millennia. It is these links that are bringing us
closer to the day when the first real world history of mankind can be
written.

Chapter XI

POSTSCRIPT
ON BAT CREEK

R O M A N C O N T A C T with America around A.D. 200 is indicated by the head found *in situ* by archeologists at the pyramid of Calixtlahuaca in Mexico (see the article by R. Heine-Geldern, in the bibliography). This piece of solid evidence adds credence to earlier accidental finds such as the Roman coins, with Latin inscriptions, found in the American Southeast since over a century and a half ago, as documented by John Haywood, *Natural and Aboriginal History of Tennessee,* George Wilson, Nashville, Tennessee, 1823 (republished by Mary U. Rothrock, McCowat-Mercer Press, Jackson, Tenn., 1959). Haywood identified coins of the Antonines and Commodus (second century A.D.). Other contacts with the Roman Mediterranean of the second century A.D. have meanwhile come to light in Kentucky, where inscribed Hebrew coins of Bar Kokhba's rebellion against Rome (A.D. 132–135) were dug up in Louisville, Hopkinsville and Clay City. The assorted coins were found at different times and in widely separated areas: at Louisville in 1932, at Clay City in 1952, and Hopkinsville in 1967. These coins have been examined and identified by Professor Israel T. Naamani of the University of Louisville (see *The Courier-Journal,* Louisville, of July 12, 1953, March 14, 1967, March 20, 1967). There is no difficulty in identifying these Bar Kokhba coins. The Clay City coin was sent to the late Professor Ralph Marcus of the University of Chicago who had no trouble in reading "Simon" (Bar Kokhba's personal name) on one side, and "Year 2 of the Freedom of

Bar Kokhba Coins.

Bar Kokhba Coins.

Israel" (i.e., A.D. 133) on the other. The Hebrew script is quite familiar from Jewish coins of the Roman period down to A.D. 135; see The-
odore Reinach, *Jewish Coins,* Argonaut, Chicago, 1966; Yaᶜakov
Meshorer, *Jewish Coins of the Second Temple Period,* Am Hassefer,
Tel-Aviv, 1967.

Neither the Latin nor the Hebrew coins from our Southeast made
any impression on archeologists or historians, partly because the coins
were not excavated by professionals. However, unbeknownst to the
academic world, a Hebrew inscription of Roman date (probably
around A.D. 135) was scientifically excavated in Tennessee and published by Cyrus Thomas in the *Twelfth Annual Report of the Bureau
of Ethnology to the Secretary of the Smithsonian Institution 1890–'91,*
Government Printing Office, Washington, D.C., 1894, pp. 392–394
and figures 272, 273. Thomas, without understanding the nature of
the writing, published the text upside down on p. 394 and quite erroneously surmised it to be in the Cherokee script.

The inscribed stone, which is the property of the Smithsonian Institution, was excavated in an unrifled burial mound 28 feet in diameter
and 5 feet high. Cyrus Thomas describes the find as follows: "Nothing
of interest was discovered until the bottom was reached, where nine
skeletons were found lying on the original surface of the ground, surrounded by dark colored earth. These were disposed as shown on p.
166. No. 1 lying at full length with the head south, and close by, parallel with it, but with the head north, was No. 2. On the same level were
seven others, all lying close side by side, with heads north and in a
line. All were badly decayed. No relics were found with any but No. 1,
immediately under the skull and jaw bones of which were two copper
bracelets, an engraved stone, a small drilled fossil, a copper bead, a
bone implement, and some small pieces of polished wood. The earth
about the skeletons was wet and the pieces of wood soft and colored
green by contact with the copper bracelets. The bracelets had been
rolled in something, probably bark, which crumbled away when they
were taken out. The engraved stone lay partially under the back part
of the skull and was struck by the steel prod used in probing."

The arrangement of the nine skeletons is interesting. Because all the
objects were under the head of No. 1, it looks as though he was the
chief to whom the stone belonged. No. 2, lying beside him, might be

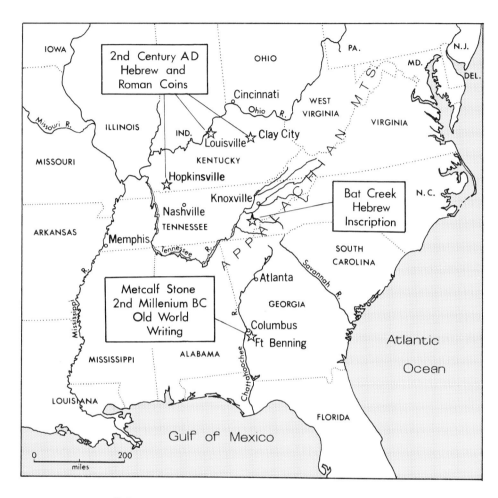

SOUTHEAST UNITED STATES

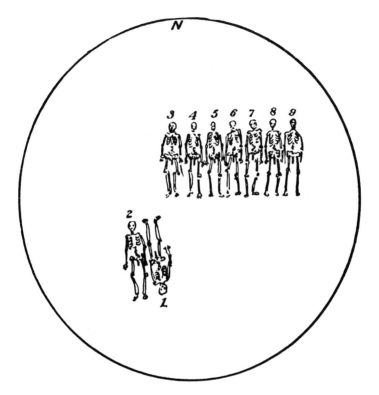

Disposition of the Skeletons, Burial #3, Bat Creek, Tennessee.

his wife, while the seven others (Nos. 3–9) in a separate row might be attendants. This would imply the custom of killing the retinue to accompany a dead chief in the afterlife.

Before anything constructive could be done with the text, someone had to turn it right side up. Henriette Mertz, a patent lawyer in Chicago, not only did this but recognized the script as "Phoenician" (which includes ancient Hebrew letter-forms) on p. 130 of her book *The Wine Dark Sea* (published by the author, Box 207, Old Post Office, Chicago 60690), 1964. Her suggestion made no impression on Semitists partly because her facsimile and identifications were right in the case of only two letters. Unfortunately, errors often blind scholars to the correct elements, which in the last analysis are the only ones that really matter.

It remained for Joseph B. Mahan, Jr., Director of Education and Research at the Columbus (Georgia) Museum of Arts and Crafts, to realize independently that if the Bat Creek Stone is turned right side up, its script is plainly Canaanite. Dr. Mahan noted that a sequence of letters (which we can now read as LYHWD) on the Stone corresponded to letters on a chart of the Canaanite alphabet which he found in the *Cambridge Ancient History*. He communicated his discovery to me with an excellent photograph made specially for him by the Smithsonian. The obvious advantage of a good photograph over an inaccurate facsimile enabled me for the first time to work on the Stone with confidence. Though the priority of discovery goes to Dr. Mertz, it was Dr. Mahan's independent rediscovery which led to results.

The paleographic key to the date of the inscription is the shape of the W which occurs on the Hebrew coins of the Bar Kokhba revolt. Moreover, the style of embellishing the letters with a little drilled hole (as at the top of the L and Y) typifies Hebrew coins of the Roman period. Once the date and style are established, the fifth letter of the five-letter sequence can only be D (and not an imperfectly drawn aleph), and an aleph characteristic of the coins (which looks entirely different from the D) actually appears below the Y. The sequence LYHWD means "for (L) Judea (YHWD)." Possibly the traces immediately following LHWD are the upper left remnant of an M, in which case the text LYHWDM would mean "for the Judeans." But by itself YHWD can stand for the Judean Commonwealth, and was so used since the Achaemenian Period.

The Bat Creek Inscription.

Facsimile of Bat Creek Inscription.

The two letters to the right of the word divider are problematic. It has been suggested that they be read QṢ "end." If this should prove correct, the meaning would be "The End of Days," marking not only the termination of this painful historic eon, but the beginning of the Golden or Messianic Age. This meaning of QṢ is in the Old Testament (Daniel 12:4), in the Dead Sea Scrolls from Qumran, and persists into later Judaism including Maimonides' formulation of the Thirteen Principles of the Faith. The sense of QṢ · LYHWD(M) would thus be "The Golden Age for the Jews" ushering in a new era of bliss. The aleph written below would stand for the numeral "1" and the inscription would be translated "Year 1 of the Golden Age for the Jews."

The difficulty in reading QṢ is twofold. The Ṣ resembles the cursive Ṣ in the Dead Sea Scrolls from Qumran, but not the lapidary Ṣ that is also used on the coins. Careful method requires that we read every letter within the same system unless there is some compelling reason to posit one cursive-type letter in this particular context; and there is no such reason. Furthermore the Q should not have the little horizontal stroke at the base; Q with such a stroke occurs nowhere on the coins. My student Robert Stieglitz proposed the reading ZQ, which merits consideration. The Z occurs on a chart of the Hebrew coin script (M. A. Levy, *Geschichte der jüdischen Münzen,* Nies'sche Buchdruckerei, Leipzig, 1862, p. 137), and the Q is paralleled on a number of coins. ZQ means a "spark, planet, comet." Simon's epithet "Bar Kokhba," means "Son of the Star." Accordingly "The Comet" could well refer to the Messianic figure expected to inaugurate and preside over the Golden Age. The sense of the text would be essentially the same: "Year 1: Comet (= Messiah) of the Jews."

The spelling of YHWD with a consonant (W) standing for a vowel (*u*) is typically Hebrew. (The Phoenicians would have written it simply YHD.) This confirms the Jewish nature of the inscription obviously implied by the very name YHWD.

The letter-forms may be dated about A.D. 100 with enough leeway to cover refugees from Judea fleeing from the Romans during the First (A.D. 66–70) or Second (A.D. 132–135) rebellions. However, the unearthing of Bar Kokhba coins in the adjacent state of Kentucky tips the scale in favor of a date around A.D. 135 for the migration of Jewish refugees, who sought the Messianic Order in America after their

LETTER FORMS

| BAT CREEK | MODERN HEBREW | CLOSEST FORMS ON MESHORER'S *Jewish Coins* (##5–36 = MACCABEAN, ##148–164 = FIRST REBELLION, ##165–215 = SECOND REBELLION) OR OTHER SOURCES AS INDICATED |

I. IDENTIFIED LETTERS

Ŧ Χ F (#148), Ŧ (##149, 169, 179, 180)

＜ ד ㄑ (##28, 152)

Ⴢ ה Ⴈ (##27, 154)

Ⴤ ו Ⴤ (#154)

∿ י ∿ (#159), ∿ (#154)

L ל L (##148, 200, 201)

II. PROBLEMATIC LETTERS

| ｜ ｜ (##18A, 22, 23)

𝒫

ד ₣ ₣ (LEVY, *JÜDISCHE MÜNZEN*, P. 137)

OR

ז ₹ (#154)

ז ₹ (#148), ₹ (#164), ₹ (#151)

OR

ע CF. CURSIVE FORMS IN THE QUMRAN MANUAL OF DISCIPLINE:

ע (1:6), ע (4:2) & HABAKKUK COMMENTARY: ע (1:14

ע (4:11)

III. POSSIBLE RESTORATION
OF BROKEN LETTER

ṃ מ ṃ (#30) & THE OLDER FORM ṃ (LEVY, *OP. CIT.*, P. 136)

hope in the Old World had been shattered. This was not the last wave of the Old World immigrants looking for a better life on these shores. Nor was it the first.

The Bat Creek inscription inscribed in Roman antiquity is not a souvenir imported from the Old World after 1492 to gratify some Cherokee chief's love of East Mediterranean archeology—a love so great that he took the inscribed stone with him for eternity in the next life. The script was not even deciphered until the nineteenth century. Trying to explain away the Bat Creek evidence as anything other than American contact with Palestine around the second century A.D. can only amount to obscurantism that no sensible scholar or layman should elect. The Atlantic was crossed long before the Vikings, by different peoples during different centuries. The significance of the excavations at Bat Creek is that they attest inscriptionally and archeologically a migration in early Christian times from Judea to our Southeast.

APPENDIXES

NOTES

1. "Hypostyle" means that the superstructure is held up by columns. In Egypt, and at Mesoamerican sites such as Chichén Itzá, the effect may be described as "a forest of columns."

2. Actually, pre-Columbian wheeled ceramic toy animals have been found in Mesoamerica, in Veracruz and other parts of Mexico and in El Salvador. Gordon F. Ekholm et al. (*Ancient Mexico and Central America,* The American Museum of Natural History, New York, 1970, p. 75) have appraised the situation judiciously: "The occurrence of these wheeled animals is extraordinary, for the use of wheeled vehicles was otherwise completely unknown in the New World. They have been explained as an independent invention of the principle of the wheel. But it appears more likely that they are the result of influences from the civilizations of Asia, where small wheeled animals very similar to these were widespread in ancient times." To this day hordes of Maya walk and carry merchandise on their backs, to and from Chichicastenango, every Thursday and Sunday. The fact that they use no wheeled vehicles despite four and a half centuries of close contact with Europeans shows how tenaciously people may cling to old habits and resist even the most useful innovations.

3. Dennis Lou delivered a paper on "Chinese Cultural Influence in Pre-Columbian America" before the International Congress of Orientalists, at Ann Arbor, Michigan, in August 1967. Lou has collected actual Chinese inscriptions on pre-Columbian objects as well as pointed out striking cultural analogues between China and ancient America. On pp. 3–4 of his abstract, Lou concludes: "Asian parallels in America may be roughly divided into two periods: The first period running from about 1000 B.C. or even earlier to the beginning of the Christian era, and the second period

from the beginning of the Christian Era to about the 10th Century A.D. The parallels of the first period were dominated by Chinese cultural traits of the Shang and Han dynasties. In the second period, the parallels were dominated by influence from India, Southeast Asia, Indonesia or Polynesia.

"An interesting point is that before the Han period, there was a tremendous amount of shipbuilding and sea-faring activities along the Eastern China Coast. Great naval squadrons with double canoes and double-decked boats and famous sailors were widely recorded in Chinese literature of the Ch'un Chiu period (8th to 5th Century B.C.). One record of the first century B.C. stated that the King of Yueh (a kingdom located around today's Kungtung Province) ordered 2,800 members from his fleet of double-deck boats to go ashore and cut cedar and pine trees for the purposes of building naval vessels (Yueh-chu-shu, bol. 8). After the Han period (3rd Century B.C. to 3rd Century A.D.), Southern China was finally put under the control of the central government of China, and the sea-faring activities gradually disappeared. From this time on China saw the coming of traders from India, Arabia, the Mediterranean Coast and Indonesia.

"At the beginning of the T'ang dynasty (6th Century A.D.), early Chinese literatures showed, sea-trading traffic began to increase. During this period, trading boats generally sailed into the South Pacific and toward the Indian Ocean. Some of these trading boats were said to have been in a voyage for one year without stopping for water and provisions, and that these boats could carry as many as a thousand passengers."

3a. The periods of pre-Columbian Mesoamerica are:

a.	Early pre-Classical	1660–1000 B.C.
b.	Middle pre-Classical	1000–600 B.C.
c.	Late pre-Classical	600 B.C.–A.D. 300
d.	Early Classical	A.D. 300–600
e.	Late Classical	A.D. 600–900
f.	Early post-Classical	A.D. 900–1300
g.	Late post-Classical	A.D. 1300–1521

Some scholars prefer "Formative" to "pre-Classical," and place Early Formative from 2500 to 1500 B.C., and Middle Formative from 1500 to 600 B.C.

4. There are different ways of explaining this phenomenon. Some authorities believe that the effect was achieved by artificial nose pieces. Others hold that the bone structure of the nose and head was intentionally warped in infancy to produce the effect desired. Whatever the explanation, the sculptures must be compared with Old World representations showing the same phenomenon. Among them are a bronze now in the Museum of Valencia, Spain, and the relief face on a Philistine sarcophagus from Beth-shan, Israel. The latter is of special interest because the Philistines were Sea

People from the Aegean, where the wide-ranging Minoan thalassocrats had previously held sway.

5. Jonathan N. Leonard, *Ancient America,* Time Incorporated, New York, 1967, p. 11.

6. Ibid., pp. 10–11.

7. Betty J. Meggers, Clifford Evans and Emilio Estrada, *Early Formative Period of Coastal Ecuador: the Valdivia and Machalilla phases (Smithsonian Contributions to Anthropology* Vol. I), Smithsonian Institution, Washington, D.C., 1965.

8. Leonard, op. cit., p. 12.

9. Among the popular books with broad perspective on this subject are: Charles Michael Boland, *They All Discovered America,* Pocket Books, Inc., New York, 1961; Constance Irwin, *Fair Gods and Stone Faces,* St. Martin's Press, New York, 1963; and Pierre Honoré, *In Quest of the White God,* Putnam, New York, 1964. A brief but well-documented and scholarly refutation of exaggerated independent inventionism has been written by Stephen C. Jett and George F. Carter, "A Comment on Rowe's 'Diffusionism and Archaeology,'" *American Antiquity,* Vol. 31, No. 6, Oct. 1966, pp. 867–870.

10. Cyrus H. Gordon, *Forgotten Scripts: How They Were Deciphered and Their Impact on Contemporary Culture,* Basic Books, New York, 1968.

11. The surviving fragments of Theopompus of Chios (born ca. 380 B.C.) have been published by Felix Jacoby, *Die Fragmente der griechischen Historiker,* Vol. II, 1929–30; reproduced photomechanically by Brill, Leiden, 1954–1969. In the *Meropis* of Theopompus, Silenus describes the Meropids as dwelling on a continent beyond Africa and the islands of the ocean, in a land with cities and where gold and silver are so common that they have less value than iron.

12. The Roman poet Rufus Festus Avienus flourished during the second half of the fourth century A.D.

13. Aristotle, *Minor Works,* edited by W. S. Helt, Loeb Classical Library, London (England) and Cambridge (Mass.), 1955.

14. Diodorus of Sicily, *Library of History,* Vol. III, edited by C. H. Oldfather, Loeb Classical Library, London (England) and Cambridge (Mass.), 1952.

15. The Greek *hēmerôn pleiónōn* should be rendered "many days" rather than "a number of days" (as Oldfather translates).

16. The *Periplus* of Hanno, which has survived in Greek translation, is the account of how a Carthaginian fleet of sixty ships carrying 30,000 people explored and colonized the west African coast, around 425 B.C. A quarter of a century earlier the Carthaginian Himilco had sailed along the coast of Western Europe; his story is told by Avienus in *Ora Maritima.*

17. Aelian (*Claudius Aelianus* ca. A.D. 170–235) states this in his *Varia Historia* 3:18 in an important excerpt from Theopompus.

18. Strabo, *Geography*, Vols. I and II, Loeb Classical Library, edited by H. L. Jones, London (England) and Cambridge (Mass.), 1959.

19. Henriette Mertz, *The Wine Dark Sea: Homer's Heroic Epic of the North Atlantic*, published by the author (Box 207, Old Post Office, Chicago 60690), 1964. Dr. Mertz's bold identifications have been attacked, often quite rudely, by critics who forget that the geographic framework within which she operates has some merits vis-à-vis theirs, which is too restricted. That her work, like all pioneering, needs serious correction is another matter. Miss Mertz, who is a patent lawyer, has also rendered a service in combating the routine branding of every Old World inscription found in America as fakery. Her professional understanding of what constitutes evidence is a valuable corrective against the die-hard negators, who rule out any unwelcome evidence as forgeries and fail to realize that unreasonable skepticism can be just as misleading as uncritical gullibility.

20. The Greeks lumped all the Northwest Semites together as "Phoenician." Some of Northwest Semitic "languages" which we carefully distinguish in our current scientific terminology are merely mutually intelligible dialects. Speakers of Hebrew and Phoenician, for example, had no trouble understanding each other. For the decipherment of Minoan as Northwest Semitic, see Cyrus H. Gordon, *Ugarit and Minoan Crete*, W. W. Norton, New York, 1966 (and paperback edition, 1967).

21. Intermittent transatlantic crossings were made from Roman times through the Renaissance, but they were kept secret. A wide variety of Roman coins have turned up in North America: too many to be accidental. Hebrew coins of Bar Kokhba's rebellion against Rome (A.D. 132–135) have been found, according to newspaper reports, at Louisville, Clay City and Hopkinsville, Kentucky. See Chapter XI.

22. Plato, Vol. VII (includes *Timaeus* and *Critias*), Loeb Classical Library, edited by R. B. Bury, London (England) and Cambridge (Mass.), 1952.

23. Plato mentions this continent (which can only be America) without more ado, for he assumes that his Greek reading public knew of its existence. On the other hand, he refers to Atlantis as hearsay from an Egyptian priest who told Solon that it had sunk 9,000 years previously. Common sense should tell us that Plato's factual reference to the continent, which he correctly describes as bordering the entire ocean on the west, is more significant than the legend he reports about a mysterious land that had disappeared nine millennia earlier.

24. Odyssey 13:172–178.

25. For a survey and background, see Hans Jensen, *Sign, Symbol and Script: An Account of Man's Efforts to Write*, Putnam, New York, 1969. The

relation between certain pre-Columbian American and Mediterranean scripts will be discussed in Chapter V, below.

26. For a detailed treatment of this subject see Hilda Lockhart Lorimer, *Homer and the Monuments,* Macmillan, London, 1950.

27. It is interesting to note that the Hebrews and even the Phoenicians have no verb meaning "to sail, navigate" but instead apply the verb *hlk* "to walk, go" to ships. Hebrew and Phoenician *oniyya* "ship" is a common Semitic noun for "implement, container, vessel" reflecting how deeply navigation is embedded in ancient life and psychology. That we use "vessel" for "ship" shows that the same holds true for our West European tradition.

28. Described by M. S. F. Hood, "The Tartaria Tablets," *Scientific American* 218, No. 5, May 1968, pp. 30–37.

29. For a recent and readable account of Egyptian literature, see Joseph Kaster, *Wings of the Falcon,* Holt, Rinehart and Winston, New York, 1968. The most convenient edition of *The Shipwrecked Sailor* in hieroglyphic Egyptian is on pp. 101–106 of A. De Buck, *Egyptian Readingbook* I, Nederlandsche Archaeologisch-Philologisch Instituut voor het Nabije Oosten, Leiden, 1948.

30. "Fingers" is a synonym of "hands" also in Hebrew and Ugaritic literatures.

31. Such matters, and their implications, are treated in Cyrus H. Gordon, *The Common Background of Greek and Hebrew Civilizations,* W. W. Norton, New York, 1965.

32. The hounds, monkeys and apes are shipped alive (like the peacocks and apes imported by Solomon's fleet to Israel). Animals and plants were in many cases introduced to distant lands in antiquity. Note D. M. Dixon, "The Transplantation of Punt Incense Trees in Egypt," *Journal of Egyptian Archaeology* 55, August 1969, pp. 55–65; and F. Nigel Hepper, "Arabian and African Frankincense Trees," ibid., pp. 66–72.

33. The pyramid burial at Palenque in Mexico has too many Egyptian and Near Eastern features for purely accidental parallelism. For instance, the Palenque sarcophagus flares out at the base like Egyptian and Phoenician coffins so designed for stability when stood on end. The feature is retained nonfunctionally by the horizontally laid Palenque sarcophagus.

34. See G. Posener, "Le Canal du Nil à la Mer Rouge avant les Ptolémées," *La Chronique d'Égypte* 13, 1938, pp. 259–273.

35. Robert Heine-Geldern, "Ein römischer Fund aus dem vorkolumbischen Mexico," *Anzeiger der Oesterreichischen Akademie der Wissenschaften, Philosophische-historische Klasse* 98, 1961, pp. 117–119.

36. Mendel Peterson of the Smithsonian Institution, in Washington, D.C., who is preparing this hoard of coins for publication, has kindly showed me the material.

37. Armando Cortesão, *The Nautical Chart of 1424 and the Early Discovery and Cartographical Representation of America,* University of Coimbra, Coimbra, 1954.

38. Gerald S. Hawkins, *Stonehenge Decoded,* Doubleday, Garden City, N.Y., 1965. Stonehenge, which embodies not only architectural but also astronomical principles, is not an isolated structure; for near it are other megalithic sites such as Avebury (which covers much more area than Stonehenge), Woodhenge and others. Moreover, features of Stonehenge link it to distant megalithic edifices, e.g., the horseshoe formations known also from the Hagar Qim and Tarxien temples on Malta. The numerous double axes incised on the Stonehenge monoliths, and the Mycenaean-type dagger carved on one of them, connect the structure with the Minoan world. It is also worth noting that Egyptian blue faience beads of about 1400 B.C. have been found in barrows at Stonehenge, linking the burials there with Egypt in the Amarna Age (late fifteenth and early fourteenth centuries B.C.). The international Amarna Age was therefore not restricted to the Near East, but reached out into the Atlantic.

39. Note that Hesiod (*Works and Days,* Loeb Classical Library, edited by Hugh G. Evelyn-White, London, England, and Cambridge, Mass., 1954, pp. 12–14, lines 158–160) attributes a worldwide distribution to the Heroic Age which he describes as "more just and virtuous, a godlike race of heroic men, who are called demigods, the race preceding (our iron race) over the boundless earth." The Hebrews have a similar tradition for they too regarded "the heroes who of old were renowned men" as demigods (Genesis 6:4).

40. Berossos transmits this tradition. He was a Babylonian priest who wrote in Greek a work called *Babyloniaca* during the reign of Antiochus I Soter (281–262 B.C.). The passage in question has been preserved by Eusebius (*Chronicon* I); it is translated and annotated by Erich Ebeling in *Altorientalische Texte zum Alten Testament,* edited by Hugo Gressmann, Berlin and Leipzig, 2nd ed., 1926, pp. 146–147.

41. Rome absorbed these ideas at an early stage; through Vergil, they became entrenched as standard doctrine. See Cyrus H. Gordon, "Vergil and the Near East," *Ugaritica* VI, Paul Geuthner, Paris, 1969, pp. 267–288.

42. The foundations firmly laid by Darwin and Wallace, establishing what was to become known as the origin of species, "excited very little attention, and the only published notice of them . . . was by Professor Haughton of Dublin, whose verdict was that all that was new in them was false, and what was true was old" (*The Darwin Reader,* edited by Marston Bates and Philip S. Humphrey, Charles Scribner's Sons, New York, 1956, p. 24).

43. A well-illustrated survey has been published by Gale Sieveking, *apud* Edward Bacon, *Vanished Civilizations of the Ancient World,* McGraw-Hill,

New York, and Thames and Hudson, London, 1963; see "The Migration of the Megaliths," pp. 299–322.

44. A pamphlet by Celia Topp, *Pre-Historic Malta and Gozo,* Progress Press, Valetta, Malta (n.d.), is a handy guide with photographs. A fuller description of a specific site is T. Zammit, *The Copper Age Temples of Hal-Tarxien,* 4th ed., Malta, 1966. For finds connected with the Malta temples see D. H. Trumps' official guide *National Museum of Malta: Archaeological Section* (n.d.).

45. The sheer number of megalithic structures on Minorca is staggering; see J. Mascaro Pasarius (ed.), *Monumentos Prehistóricos y Protohistóricos de la Isla de Menorca,* Gráficas Miramar, Palma de Mallorca, 1967.

46. Comprehensively covered in Edward Bacon's *Vanished Civilizations of the Ancient World,* cited above.

47. This is confirmed by other links with the Near East of the Late Bronze Age; e.g., the discovery of Egyptian blue faience beads in the barrows around Stonehenge, as mentioned above.

48. See the photograph of the "Round Zodiac" of Dendera on the plate opposite p. 217 in Giorgio de Santillana and Hertha von Dechend, *Hamlet's Mill,* Gambit, Boston, 1969.

49. Spyridon Marinatos and Max Hirmer, *Crete and Mycenae,* Harry N. Abrams (n.d.); see plates 72 and 73 for both sides of the Disc.

50. T. Zammit, *The Copper Age Temples of Hal-Tarxien,* fig. 13.

51. The animal attributes of Thueris are a mixture of crocodile and hippopotamus features.

52. Our indebtedness to ancient Babylonia is not limited to the nomenclature of the planets; when modern astronomers, mathematicians and cartographers divide the circle into 360°, they are following in the footsteps of their predecessors in Babylonia.

53. Babylonian Talmud, *Avodah Zarah,* Vilna Edition, p. 54b.

54. We are not dealing with primitive peoples such as the aborigines of Australia or the Amazon jungles, whose culture has no scientific component.

55. Such numbers have long histories as specific lucky or unlucky numerals.

56. See Eleazar L. Sukenik, *The Ancient Synagogue of Beth Alpha,* University Press, Jerusalem, 1932; and *Ancient Synagogues in Palestine and Greece* (1930 Schweich Lecture), British Academy, London, 1934. For a more recent discussion of the Beth Alpha synagogue and its mosaics, with illustrations, see Bernard Goldman, *The Sacred Portal,* Wayne State University Press, Detroit, 1966. For superb illustrations, see Meyer Schapiro and Michael Avi-Yonah, *Israel: Ancient Mosaics,* New York Graphic Society (by arrangement with UNESCO), copyright 1960 in Paris.

57. Hopefully this scroll will be published before long.

58. This literature, in translation and with notes, is well (but not exhaustively) covered in James B. Pritchard (editor), *Ancient Near Eastern Texts,* 2nd ed., Princeton University Press, Princeton, 1955, with additions in the same editor's *The Ancient Near East: Supplementary Texts and Pictures Relating to the Old Testament,* Princeton, 1969.

59. James L. Breasted, *The Edwin Smith Surgical Papyrus,* 2 vols., University of Chicago Press, Chicago, 1930.

60. Maurice B. Gordon, *Aesculapius Comes to the Colonies,* Argosy-Antiquarian Ltd., New York, 1969.

61. The Yuchis now adjust the date, whenever necessary, to tie in with a week-end.

62. When I showed a cast of the Metcalf Stone to Professor Stanislav Segert of the University of Prague, his immediate reaction was that the script is derived from the Aegean of the second millennium B.C. and marks a transition from syllabary to alphabet.

63. Pierre Honoré, *Ich Fand den Weissen Gott,* Scheffler, Frankfort am Main, 1965, p. 121.

64. Thus the distinctive Minoan *qe*-sign is identical with a Mayan glyph.

65. Rather prophetically, Henri Frankfort (*Cylinder Seals,* Macmillan, New York and London, 1939, p. 18, etc.) described certain seal designs as "heraldic." Cylindrical seals are characteristic of Mesopotamian culture, and their very presence in ancient America calls for a detailed investigation.

66. For an illustrated description of writing throughout the world, see David Diringer, *The Alphabet: A Key to the History of Mankind,* 3rd ed., 2 volumes, Funk & Wagnalls, New York, 1968.

67. Thus the horn comes in as the syllable *we,* the leonine head as *ma,* etc.

68. Cyrus H. Gordon, *Homer and Bible,* Ventnor Publishers, Ventnor, N.J., reprinting of 1967, p. 71 (§180).

69. Moran and Kelley (pp. 69–123) would derive the early shapes of such letters from the forms of the constellations they designate. This possibility deserves careful investigation.

70. The apparent discrepancy of *c* (pronounced *k*) instead of *g* in this position is due to the Etruscans who did not distinguish *k* from *g* phonetically.

71. Not *th* as in "thing"; but like *t+h* as in "set him."

72. Originally *i* and *j* were the same letter; thus in Latin "Julius" can be spelled *Iulius* or *Julius.* When vocalic, *i* was obligatory; when consonantal, *j* could be used.

73. The Greek letter *ksi,* pronounced like our *x,* not only represents the way the Greeks heard the Semitic sound that is usually transliterated *s,* but occurs in the same position in the alphabet.

74. The Semitic consonant *c* does not occur in Greek; the Greeks heard it as a vowel that they recorded as *o*, and it appears in the same position as ^c in the alphabet.

75. Called *koppa* in Greek, to be distinguished from *kappa* above.

76. Neither Latin nor Greek has a distinctive *sh* sound. Phoenician-Hebrew *sh* therefore comes into Greek and Latin as *s*. The Ugaritic *ṯ* (pronounced like *th* in "thing") does not occur among the phonemes of Phoenician or Hebrew, but comes into those languages as *sh*.

77. The Piri Reis map was made of regional maps. Two maps of the Amazon were erroneously included when the large map was compiled. There are numerous problems in detail in the study of this and other ancient maps, but the conclusions deduced by Hapgood deserve careful consideration. For example, he fixes the focal point of the ancient map maker (corresponding to our Greenwich, England) in Upper Egypt.

78. Herodotus 4:196. Note also that the Carthaginians, after setting out their wares on the shore, attracted the attention of the natives by sending up smoke as a signal from aboard their vessel. Such signals were also part of the "international language."

79. 2 Kings 18:26.

80. Explained in Cyrus H. Gordon, "Hebrew 'HDYM = ILTÊNÛTU 'Pair,' " *Sepher Segal,* Israel Society for Biblical Research, Jerusalem, 1965, pp. 5–9; and *Ugaritic Textbook,* Pontifical Biblical Institute, Rome, 1967, p. 43 (§7.8).

81. See Waldemar Fenn, *Gráfica Prehistórica de España y el Origen de la Cultura Europea,* Mahon, Minorca, 1950.

82. As Vincent H. Cassidy has aptly put it (in an unpublished address entitled "An Approach to Pre-Columbian Contacts with the New World: Old World Records and New World Sites") : "Plato's 'Atlantis' is, understandably, receiving much current attention; but his 'other continent' receives studied neglect."

83. Cyrus H. Gordon, *Evidence for the Minoan Language,* Ventnor Publishers, Ventnor, N.J., 1966.

84. The subject as a whole is covered by Sabatino Moscati, *The World of the Phoenicians,* Praeger, New York and Washington, D.C., 1968.

85. 1 Samuel 13:19–22.

86. Herodotus 7:89.

87. 1 Kings 9:27 mentions that the men Hiram supplied for the Red Sea fleet knew *the* sea. If the definite article in the Hebrew text has a specific meaning, it can only refer to the Red Sea. Pilots have to know the particular waters on which they are sailing.

88. 1 Kings 10:22.

89. 1 Kings 9:28.

90. The Gold Coast of Africa? A later Carthaginian mission along the coast of West Africa (by Hanno around 425 B.C.) is generally held to have been launched in quest of gold (Moscati, op. cit., p. 184).

91. 1 Kings 10:22.

92. Conceivably, boats in a number of periods could have sailed between the Red and Mediterranean seas via the Nile and a canal connecting it with the Gulf of Suez. However, this would not make sense for any power that controlled ports on both seas simultaneously, especially since it would run into unnecessary complications (including tolls) in Egypt.

93. Genesis 10:29.

94. Genesis 10:4; 1 Chronicles 1:7. The genealogy in 1 Chronicles 7:6–10, however, associates Tarshish with the Hebrew tribe of Benjamin. There would be nothing strange if the East Mediterranean ties with Tarshish included Semites as well as Greeks. It is interesting to note that one of the Seven Princes who served as intimate counselors of Xerxes was named Tarshish (Esther 1:14). Since Esther 10:1 attributes an overseas empire to Xerxes ("King Xerxes imposed tribute on the land and the islands of the sea"), it is conceivable that the Achaemenian Empire at its height had interests in Tarshish. For naming people after distant provinces of an empire, compare the Roman name "Britannicus."

95. The evidence is assembled by Cyrus H. Gordon, "Vergil and the Near East," *Ugaritica VI,* Paul Geuthner, Paris, 1969, pp. 267–288; note pp. 284–287.

96. 2 Chronicles 8:2–6.

97. For Phoenician expansionism, see Moscati, op. cit., p. 94ff.

98. Ibid., pp. 181–184.

99. See "brazil" in *The Oxford English Dictionary,* Clarendon Press, Oxford, 1933, vol. I, pp. 1066–1067.

100. Joseph M. Solá-Solé, "Semitic Elements in Ancient Hispania," *Catholic Biblical Quarterly* 29, No. 3, July 1967, pp. 181–188; see pp. 184–185.

101. Salvador de Madariaga, *Christopher Columbus: Being the Life of the Very Magnificent Lord Don Cristóbal Colón,* Macmillan, New York, 1940; see index under "Brazil" for the Island of Brazil and the Seven Cities.

102. Renato Castelo Branco, *O Piauí: A terra o homen o meio,* 2nd ed., Quatro Artes, São Paulo, Brazil, 1970. See pp. 161–178 on the " 'Sete Cidades'— Ruínas Fenícias no Piauí?"

103. *Atlas of the World,* 2nd ed., National Geographic Society, Washington, D.C., 1966, p. 70.

104. Now spelled "Paraíba."

105. I.e., they are commonly attested in Northwest Semitic inscriptions.

106. I have documented this, and the following, and still other points in *Orientalia* 37, 1968, pp. 75–80, 425–436, 461–463.

107. The fact that the mariners name the land they are in, and through the name indicate its chief mineral resource, shows that they were not lost on an unknown shore.

108. Scientific exactness is approximated particularly in what is known as "phonetic law." For example, the sound that is written *z* (pronounced *ts*) in German regularly appears as *t* in normal English cognates; *zu* = "to" or "too," *zwei* = "two," *zehn* = "ten," *zwanzig* = "twenty," *Zeichen* = "token," *schwarz* = "swart," etc. Somewhat as in the exact sciences, one could "predict" that German *Zoll* corresponds to English "toll."

109. Ultimately, "brother" and "friar" are related, for both are derived from the same Indo-European word; compare, for example, Persian *bradâr* "brother." "Brother" is the normal English cognate; "friar" is Norman French (= modern French *frère*) and was borrowed in the ecclesiastical sense of "brother." The other three words have nothing to do in origin with their translational equivalents, but show the impact of the French on England in cuisine. "Chef" means "head, chief" in the sense of "chief cook." The rustic British continued to talk about "cooks" and "sheep" and "cows"; but refined cuisine called for "chef" and "mutton" and "beef" (in modern French *chef, mouton,* and *bœuf*).

110. The photographs of terra-cotta portraits assembled by Von Wuthenau (op. cit.) show this beyond any shadow of doubt.

111. Specifically the Piri Reis map records the east coast of South America realistically, showing that the exploration was effected by transatlantic mariners. The rivers whose names begin with "Para-" flow into the Atlantic.

112. Frankfort observes that "in Sargonid times the cylinder often shows a slight concavity" (*Cylinder Seals,* p. 8; see also pl. II:h).

113. Frankfort, ibid. (pp. 18, 24, 26, 27, 85, 89, 91), actually calls such designs "heraldic" (starting with the Uruk Age before 3000 B.C.) without realizing the historic importance this fact would assume.

114. John L. Sorenson has prepared an impressive monograph entitled "The Significance of an Apparent Relationship Between the Ancient Near East and Mesoamerica," containing numerous interlocking parallels between Mesopotamia and Mesoamerica. He has published an abstract in *Dialogue* 4, No. 2, Summer 1969, pp. 80–94.

115. "Nahuatl" designates the language of the Aztecs, still spoken by many Indians in Mexico.

116. The carved bone is in the museum at Tikal. An enlarged painting of the scene is displayed on the museum wall. Just as Thueris (as already noted) has mixed animal attributes derived from the hippopotamus as well as the

crocodile, her American counterpart may have attributes affected by the native iguana. Art historians, linguists and zoologists must pool their resources to refine the definition(s) of *cipac-tli* and its reflexes in art.

117. I am indebted to Gordon Whittaker, an undergraduate at Brandeis University, for his unpublished essay on "Similarities Between Nahuatl and Old World Vocabulary." Some of the Nahuatl words and their Old World counterparts were first called to my attention by Whittaker, whose linguistic and historic acumen at an early age inspire confidence in his academic future.

118. It was quite independent of the Nahuatl evidence that I reconstructed *iwa(-n)* in Semitic (*Ugaritic Textbook,* Pontifical Biblical Institute, Rome, 1967, pp. 110–111). David Kelley informs me that enclitic *-ma* also means "and" in Nahuatl; compare *-ma* with the same meaning, syntax and enclitic character in Semitic, especially in Akkadian.

119. Note that the augment *o-* is prefixed to the preterite in the following paradigm of the indicative verb (Juan Luna Cardénas, *Compendio de grammatica Nahuatl,* 2nd ed., Aztekatl, Mexico City, 1939, p. 28):

Present	Preterite	Imperfect
ni-huitz	*o-ni-huitz-a*	*ni-huitz-a*
"I come"	"I came"	"I was coming"
ti-huitz	*o-ti-huitz-a*	*ti-huitz-a*
"thou comest"	"thou camest"	"thou wast coming"
ye-huitz	*o - huitz-a*	*huitz-a*
"he comes"	"he came"	"he was coming"
ti-huitz-e	*o-ti-huitz-ah*	*ti-huitz-ah*
"we come"	"we came"	"we were coming"
an-huitz-e	*o-an-huitz-ah*	*an-huitz-ah*
"ye come"	"ye came"	"ye were coming"
huitz-e	*o - huitz-ah*	*huitz-ah*
"they come"	"they came"	"they were coming"

Compare prefixed *o-* in Nahuatl to indicate the preterite tense with prefixed *e-* in Greek *e-paídeu-on* "I instructed" (vs. the present *paideú-ō* "I instruct"). At the same time, the indication of person by prefixes (*ni-* "I," *ti-* "thou," *ye-* "he") is alien to Indo-European, but regular in Semitic. Compare Hebrew *ti-shmōr* "thou wilt guard" vs. *yi-shmōr* "he will guard" or *te-gaddēl* "thou wilt enlarge" vs. *ye-gaddēl* "he will enlarge." Accordingly, we are confronted not merely by a typological parallel but specifically by *t-* "thou" and *y-* "he" to indicate the same persons in the Nahuatl and Semitic verbal systems. We must therefore think about linguistic alliance at the morphological as well as lexical level embracing Indo-European and Semitic (as well as other families of languages) in Nahuatl. Such factors will help us probe the twofold Biblical tradition that Tarshish was not only settled by Indo-Europeans (Greeks according to Genesis 10:4; and possibly also Persians according to Esther 1:14) but also by Semites (specifically Benjaminites in 1 Chronicles 7:10).

120. T. S. Denison, *The Primitive Aryans of America,* Denison, Chicago, 1908, p. 7. A one-sided approach led Denison into the fallacy that Nahuatl was Indo-European "in vocabulary and in verb conjugation" (p. 9). When he published his book in 1908, the phenomenon of "linguistic alliance" was not yet understood.

121. Gordon Whittaker notes the settling of Greeks on the great continent beyond the Atlantic, according to Plutarch, *De Facie Quae in Orbe Lunae Apparet,* section 26. It is also interesting to note that Sertorius (Plutarch, *Lives,* Loeb Classical Library, Vol. VIII, edited by Bernadotte Perrin, Heinemann (London) and Putnam (New York), section 8, pp. 20–23) on the Atlantic coast of Spain met sailors who had returned from two Atlantic islands 10,000 stadia from Africa. The text goes on to state the widely held belief that Homer's abode of the blessed (Odyssey 4:563–568) was situated there.

122. If the name of the Mexican rain god Tlaloc proves to be derived from Semitic *ṭll* "dew," it will constitute an important link with the Semitic Near East. Baal, otherwise known as Had(a)d is the god of rain and dew (*ṭll*); cf. *Ugaritic Textbook,* pp. 406–407, §19.1037. This link with the Near East is supported iconographically for Tlaloc and Baal are both represented as holding aloft a bolt of lightning (see Irwin, op. cit., pp. 172–173).

123. Roman influence in America is particularly well attested ca. 2nd century A.D.; see Chapter XI.

124. Some of the following river names may well begin with the same *par(a):* Parabel' (USSR), Paravani (Ozero, USSR), Parbati (India), Parbig (USSR), Pare (India), Paren' (USSR), Paria (Utah), etc.

125. The standard work on the Mayan inscriptions is J. Eric S. Thompson, *Maya Hieroglyphic Writing: Introduction,* Carnegie Institution of Washington, Washington, D.C., 1950.

126. Dennis Wingsou Lou, "Transpazifische Beziehungen in vorkolumbischer Zeit," *Umschau in Wissenschaft und Technik,* Frankfort am Main, 1966, Heft 5, pp. 145–146.

127. The basic study is Stefan Przeworski, *Syria* 11, 1930, pp. 133–145. Other specimens have been found since then; e.g., one in the summer of 1932 at the Judean site of Tell Beit Mirsim while I was a member of the field staff. See further G. Ernest Wright, *Biblical Archaeology,* p. 142, fig. 142.

128. A fine specimen is on display in the Columbus Museum of Arts and Crafts

(Columbus, Georgia). I have seen other examples in private homes including the Stavenhagen collection in Mexico City.

129. The Egyptian hieroglyph meaning "to offer" or "an offering" is an arm extended with an object held in the hand.

130. A United Press International dispatch from Moscow on July 11, 1970 (printed in *The New York Times,* Sunday, July 12, 1970), points to tobacco and maps as evidence for Far East links with ancient America. "A Soviet scientific report has suggested that it was really the Asians who discovered America.

"The new challenge to Columbus rests partly on ancient Tibetan maps and partly on the use of tobacco among Asians more than a thousand years before the birth of Jesus.

"In reporting the findings of Lev Gumilev and Bronislav Kuznetsov, who were described as Leningrad specialists in Oriental antiquity, *Tass,* the Soviet press agency, said Tuesday that 'the honor of discovery of the Americas possibly belongs to ancient Asian adventurers.'

"The agency said the specialists interpreted references in ancient Tibetan maps to a 'green land lying far across the Eastern Sea' as meaning America.

" 'This guess,' Tass added, 'is substantiated by the noteworthy fact that the purely American word "tobacco" penetrated a number of Oriental languages and dialects in hoary antiquity.' "

This report is of positive interest, though to speak of men from any one part of the Old World as the only "discoverers" of America runs counter to the evidence encompassed in this book.

131. Constance Irwin, op. cit., lists an impressive number of metallurgical techniques shared by the Old and New Worlds in pre-Columbian antiquity. A striking example is *mise en couleur* which "involves casting an object of an alloy of gold and copper, then treating the surface with acid to dissolve the copper, leaving a pure gold surface" (p. 298). Note also "hammering, embossing, annealing, welding, soldering, strap joining, incising, champlevé, cutout designs, and the manufacture of bimetallic objects" (pp. 285–286). The latter is Mrs. Irwin's quotation from the distinguished authority J. Alden Mason, *The Ancient Civilizations of Peru,* Penguin, Harmondsworth, 1957, p. 51.

132. Irwin, op. cit., pp. 280–281.

133. The situation is spelled out comprehensively by a man who has devoted his life to weaving: Herman Blum, *The Loom Has a Brain: The Wonderful World of the Weaver's Art,* Courier Printing Co., Littleton, N.H., revised 1970 edition.

134. 1 Samuel 13:19–22.

135. Kaster, op. cit., p. 246.

136. For a description of this monumental site with color plates, see William R.

Coe, *Tikal: A Handbook of the Ancient Maya Ruins* (with a guide map), 2nd ed., University of Pennsylvania, Philadelphia, 1969.

137. On this topic, I have benefited from letters kindly sent to me by Mr. Philip A. G. Howell of the Physics Department, University of Canterbury, Christchurch, New Zealand.

138. For documentation and further details, see Cyrus H. Gordon, "His Name Is 'One,' " *Journal of Near Eastern Studies* 20, No. 3, July 1970, pp. 198–199. The deification of numbers and of periods of time among the Maya is well known; see J. Eric S. Thompson, *Maya Hieroglyphic Writing: Introduction*, Carnegie Institution of Washington, 1950, pp. 12–13.

139. *Enneads* 6:9.

140. Isaiah 2:4; Micah 4:3.

141. In retrospect we know that the theoretical and applied sciences of antiquity are of more enduring value than their supposedly "relevant" applications. Around 1800 B.C., Babylonian mathematicians inscribed on tablets, which we now possess and can read, what has come down to us through more familiar channels as the "theorem of Pythagoras" concerning right-angled triangles: namely, that the square of the hypotenuse equals the sum of the squares of the other two sides. At the very time when Babylonia was laying the foundation of our modern mathematics, it was the consensus of opinion from the King down to the common people that omens portending the immediate future were far more important than the sciences themselves (i.e., which were secondarily applied to the art of divination). Babylonian anatomy concerning organs such as the sheep's liver was not popularly valued as a science, but only as a means for liver omens (hepatoscopy). King and commoner were agreed that astronomy was justified because of its astrological portents or assurances. The current emphasis on "relevance" at the expense of the sciences and other time-tested disciplines in our universities is just as fallacious as the ancient Babylonian variety.

142. William H. Prescott, *Mexico,* 2 volumes, Peter Fenelon Collier & Son, New York, 1900, vol. 2, p. 415.

143. Valuable material can be gleaned from old books written by uncritical authors who were out to prove a theory. The pickings in them may be lean, but they are nonetheless there. Such a book is James Adair's *History of the American Indian,* 1775, reedited by Samuel Cole Williams, Watauga Press, Johnson City, Tenn., 1930. Adair knew the Indians well (mainly in what is now the Southeastern U.S.A.). He based his thesis (that the Indians he knew stemmed from the Hebrews) on twenty-three arguments. For example his sixth argument deals with the counting of time by lunations and in sevens, including a sabbath. Very striking is his pointing out that the Indians had "cities of refuge" like those of the Hebrews in Numbers 35:6–34; Joshua 20 and 21; 1 Chronicles 6:57, 67. In spite of the early date at which it was written (1843), Prescott's (op. cit., vol. 2, pp.

381–410) estimate of the "Origin of the Mexican Civilization—Analogies with the Old World" is still worth reading. On the other hand, Old World archeology remains oblivious of the problem, as an examination of *Near Eastern Archaeology in the Twentieth Century,* edited by James A. Sanders, Doubleday, Garden City, New York, 1970, illustrates.

144. For documentation, see Cyrus H. Gordon, *Orientalia* 37, 1968, p. 427 (§9).

145. Joshua 6:21.

146. Joshua 8:21–26. The same holds for Hazor and the royal cities associated with it (Joshua 11:10–15).

147. 1 Samuel 15:2–3.

148. Jonathan Leonard, op. cit., p. 68.

149. See Genesis 10:5, 32. The word for "island" (*'îy*) is the same as the one used in the Brazil text to designate the New World shore. The "islands of the sea" incorporated in the Achaemenian Empire (Esther 10:1) may well include transoceanic areas.

150. Genesis 10:29.

151. Genesis 10:4.

152. On this subject we have the *magnum opus* of Joseph Needham, *Science and Civilization in China,* 4 volumes, Cambridge University Press, Cambridge, 1954–70.

153. Hapgood, op. cit., pp. 135–147. There is no point in documenting every item we cite from Hapgood with page references. His book has to be read from cover to cover, and critically digested.

154. Since our alphabet, in its traditional sequence, is attested on actual tablets from Ugarit (1400–1200 B.C.) in the Late Bronze Age, the civilization that produced the lunar lists on which our alphabet is based must be earlier.

155. It would be a mistake to attempt an exact chronology at this time, because there is so much unevaluated evidence from so many periods. And yet the reader should not be left without a judiciously circumscribed estimate of when the process was under way. The intercontinental, transoceanic contacts under discussion spanned the Bronze Age (3000–1200 B.C.). What happened earlier is less certain, and we are indebted to scholars like Hapgood for probing into the knotty problems of the prehistoric past. The entire Bronze Age, on the other hand, is historic: documented with countless cuneiform tablets, Egyptian and other texts, and impressive monuments—including the only one of the Seven Wonders still standing. The heyday of the ancient intercontinental mariners was, according to the evidence as it now stands, around the middle of the second millennium B.C. when the Minoan sea lords ruled the waves and the megalithic temples spanned the Atlantic and Mediterranean.

BIBLIOGRAPHY

Adair, James, *History of the American Indian,* 1775, reedited by Samuel Cole Williams, Watauga Press, Johnson City, Tenn., 1930.

Aristotle, *Minor Works,* ed. by W. S. Helt, Loeb Classical Library, London (England) and Cambridge (Mass.), 1955.

Atlas of the World, 2nd ed., National Geographic Society, Washington, D.C., 1966.

Augustine, *The City of God Against the Pagans,* Vol. III (Books 8 & 9), ed. by David S. Wiesen, Loeb Classical Library, Harvard University Press, Cambridge, and Wm. Heinemann, London, 1968.

Bacon, Edward (ed.), *Vanished Civilizations of the Ancient World,* McGraw-Hill, New York, and Thames and Hudson, London, 1963.

Bates, Marston, and Humphrey, Philip S. (ed.), *The Darwin Reader,* Charles Scribner's Sons, New York, 1956.

Blum, Herman, *The Loom Has a Brain: The Wonderful World of the Weaver's Art,* rev. ed., Courier Printing Co., Littleton, N.H., 1970.

Boland, Charles Michael, *They All Discovered America,* Pocket Books, Inc., New York, 1961.

Buck, A. de, *Egyptian Readingbook* I, Nederlandsche Archaeologisch-Philologisch Instituut voor het Nabije Oosten, Leiden, 1948.

Cassidy, Vincent H., "An Approach to Pre-Columbian Contacts with the New World: Old World Records and New World Sites" (an unpublished address).

Castelo Branco, Renato, *O Piauí: A terra o homen o meio,* 2nd ed., Quatro Artes, São Paulo, 1970.

Coe, William R., *Tikal: A Handbook of the Ancient Maya Ruins,* 2nd ed., University of Pennsylvania, Philadelphia, 1969.

Cohane, John Philip, *The Key,* Crown Publishers, Inc., New York, 1969.

Cortesão, Armando, *The Nautical Chart of 1424 and the Early Discovery and Cartographical Representation of America,* University of Coimbra, Coimbra, 1954.

Delekat, Lienhard, *Phönizier in Amerika: Die Echtheit der 1873 bekanntgewordenen kanaanäischen (altsidonischen) Inschrift aus Paraíba in Brasilien-nachgewiesen,* Peter Hanstein Verlag, Bonn, 1969.

Denison, T. S., *The Primitive Aryans of America,* Denison, Chicago, 1908.

Diodorus of Sicily, *Library of History,* Vol. III ed. by C. H. Oldfather, Loeb Classical Library, London (England) and Cambridge (Mass.), 1952.

Diringer, David, *The Alphabet: A Key to the History of Mankind,* 3rd. ed., 2 volumes, Funk & Wagnalls, New York, 1968.

Dixon, D. M., "The Transplantation of Punt Incense Trees in Egypt," *Journal of Egyptian Archaeology* 55, August 1969, pp. 55–65.

Ekholm, Gordon F., et al., *Ancient Mexico and Central America,* The American Museum of Natural History, New York, 1970.

Fenn, Waldemar, *Gráfica Prehistórica de España y el Origen de la Cultura Europea,* Mahon, Minorca, 1950.

Fetterman, John, "The Mystery of Newman's Ridge," *Life,* June 26, 1970, pp. 23–24. (Not in all editions.)

Frankfort, Henri, *Cylinder Seals,* Macmillan, New York and London, 1939.

Goetz, Delia, and Morley, Sylvanus G., *Popol Vuh: The Sacred Book of the Ancient Quiché Maya,* University of Oklahoma Press, Norman, 1950.

Goldman, Bernard, *The Sacred Portal,* Wayne State University Press, Detroit, 1966.

Gordon, Cyrus H., *The Common Background of Greek and Hebrew Civilizations,* Norton, New York, 1965.

————, *Evidence for the Minoan Language,* Ventnor Publishers, Ventnor, N.J., 1966.

————, *Forgotten Scripts: How They Were Deciphered and Their Impact on Contemporary Culture,* Basic Books, New York, 1968.

————, "Hebrew 'ḤDYM = ILTÊNÛTU 'Pair,' " *Sepher Segal,* Israel Society for Biblical Research, Jerusalem, 1965, pp. 5–9.

————, "His Name Is 'One,' " *Journal of Near Eastern Studies* 20, No. 3, July 1970, pp. 198–199.

————, *Homer and Bible,* Ventnor Publishers, Ventnor, N.J., printing of 1967.

————, *Ugarit and Minoan Crete,* Norton, New York, 1966.

————, *Ugaritic Textbook,* Pontifical Biblical Institute, Rome, 1967.

————, "Vergil and the Near East," *Ugaritica VI,* Paul Geuthner, Paris, 1969, pp. 267–288.

Gordon, Maurice B., *Aesculapius Comes to the Colonies,* Argosy-Antiquarian Ltd., New York, 1969.

Gressmann, Hugo (ed.), *Altorientalische Texte zum Alten Testament,* 2nd ed., Walter de Gruyter, Berlin and Leipzig, 1926.

Hapgood, Charles H., *Maps of the Ancient Sea Kings,* Chilton, Philadelphia, 1966.

Hawkins, Gerald S., *Stonehenge Decoded,* Doubleday, Garden City, New York, 1965.

Heine-Geldern, Robert, "Ein römischer Fund aus dem vorkolumbischen Mexico," *Anzeiger der Oesterreichischen Akademie der Wissenschaften, Philosophische-historische Klasse,* 98, 1961, pp. 117–119.

Hepper, F. Nigel, "Arabian and African Frankincense Trees," *Journal of Egyptian Archaeology,* 55, August 1969, pp. 66–72.

Hesiod, *Works and Days,* ed. by Hugh G. Evelyn-White, Loeb Classical Library, London (England) and Cambridge (Mass.), 1954.

Honoré, Pierre, *In Quest of the White God,* Putnam, New York, 1964.

Hood, M. S. F., "The Tartaria Tablets," *Scientific American* 218, No. 5, May 1968, pp. 30–37.

Irwin, Constance, *Fair Gods and Stone Faces,* St. Martin's Press, New York, 1963.

Jacoby, Felix, *Die Fragmente der griechischen Historiker,* Brill, Leiden, 1954–1969.

Jensen, Hans, *Sign, Symbol and Script: An Account of Man's Efforts to Write,* Putnam, New York, 1969.

Jett, Stephen C., "Diffusion versus Independent Development: The Bases of Contoversy," Chap. I in *Men Across the Sea: Problems of Pre-Columbian Old World–New World Contacts,* edited by Riley, Kelly, Remington and Rands, Univ. of Texas Press, Austin, Texas, 1971.

Jett, Stephen C., and Carter, George, "A Comment on Rowe's 'Diffusionism and Archaeology,'" *American Antiquity,* Vol. 31, No. 6, Oct. 1966, pp. 867–870.

Kaster, Joseph, *Wings of the Falcon,* Holt, Rinehart and Winston, New York, 1968.

Leonard, Jonathan N., *Ancient America,* Time Incorporated, New York, 1967.

Lorimer, Hilda Lockhart, *Homer and the Monuments,* Macmillan, London, 1950.

Lou, Dennis Wingsou, "Chinese Cultural Influence in Pre-Columbian America"; a multigraphed paper read before the International Congress of Orientalists, at Ann Arbor, Mich., in August 1967.

———, "Transpazifische Beziehungen in vorkulumbischer Zeit," *Umschau in Wissenschaft und Technik,* Frankfort am Main, 1966, Heft 5, pp. 145–146.

Luna Cardénas, Juan, *Compendio de grammatica Nahuatl,* 2nd ed., Aztekatl, Mexico City, 1939.

Madariaga, Salvador de, *Christopher Columbus: Being the Life of the Very Magnificent Lord Don Cristóbal Colón,* Macmillan, New York, 1940.

Marinatos, Spyridon, and Hirmer, Max, *Crete and Mycenae,* Harry N. Abrams, New York, n.d.

Mascaro Pasarius, J. (ed.), *Monumentos Prehistóricos y Protohistóricos de la Isla de Menorca,* Gráficas Miramar, Palma de Mallorca, 1967.

Mason, J. Alden, *The Ancient Civilizations of Peru,* Penguin, Harmondsworth, 1957.

Meggers, Betty, Evans, Clifford, and Estrada, Emilio, *Early Formative Period of Coastal Ecuador: the Valdivia and Machalilla Phases (Smithsonian Contributions to Anthropology,* Vol. I), Smithsonian Institution, Washington, D.C., 1965.

Mertz, Henriette, *The Wine Dark Sea: Homer's Heroic Epic of the North Atlantic,* published by the author, Box 207, Old Post Office, Chicago 60690, 1964.

Moran, Hugh A., and Kelley, David H., *The Alphabet and the Ancient Calendar Signs,* 2nd ed., Daily Press, 856 San Antonio Road, Palo Alto, Calif., 1969.

Moscati, Sabatino, *The World of the Phoenicians,* Praeger, New York and Washington, D.C., 1968.

Needham, Joseph, *Science and Civilization in China,* 4 volumes, Cambridge University Press, Cambridge, 1954–1970.

Oxford English Dictionary, Clarendon Press, Oxford, Vol. I, 1933.

Plato, *Timaeus* and *Critias* (in Vol. VII), ed. by R. B. Bury, Loeb Classical Library, London (England) and Cambridge (Mass.), 1952.

Plutarch, *Lives,* Vol. VIII, ed. by Bernadotte Perrin, Loeb Classical Library, Heinemann, London, and Putnam, New York.

Posener, G., "Le Canal du Nil à la Mer Rouge avant les Ptolémées," *La Chronique d'Égypte* 13, 1938, pp. 259–273.

Prescott, William H., *Mexico,* 2 volumes, Peter Fenelon Collier & Son, New York, 1900.

Pritchard, James B. (ed.), *Ancient Near Eastern Texts,* 2nd ed., Princeton University Press, Princeton, 1955, with additions in the same editor's *The Ancient Near East: Supplementary Texts and Pictures Relating to the Old Testament,* Princeton, 1969.

Przeworski, "Les Encensoirs de la Syrie du Nord et leurs Prototypes Égyptiens," *Syria* 11, 1930, pp. 133–145.

Sahagun, Bernardino de, *A History of Ancient Mexico,* translated by Fanny R. Bandelier, Fisk University Press, Nashville, Tenn., Vol. I, 1932.

Sanders, James A. (ed.), *Near Eastern Archaeology in the Twentieth Century,* Doubleday, Garden City, N.Y., 1970.

Santillana, Giorgio de, and Dechend, Hertha von, *Hamlet's Mill,* Gambit, Boston, 1969.

Schapiro, Meyer, and Avi-Yonah, Michael, *Israel: Ancient Mosaics,* New York Graphic Society (by arrangement with UNESCO), copyright 1960 in Paris.

Solá-Solé, Joseph M., "Semitic Elements in Ancient Hispania," *Catholic Biblical Quarterly* 29, No. 3, July 1967, pp. 181–188.

Sorenson, John L., "The Significance of an Apparent Relationship Between the Ancient Near East and Mesoamerica," an abstract of this unpublished monograph has been printed in *Dialogue* 4, No. 2, Summer 1969, pp. 80–94.

Strabo, *Geography,* Vols. I and II, ed. by H. L. Jones, Loeb Classical Library, London (England) and Cambridge (Mass.), 1959.

Sukenik, Eleazer L., *The Ancient Synagogue of Beth Alpha,* University Press, Jerusalem, 1932.

———, *Ancient Synagogues in Palestine and Greece* (1930 Schweich Lecture), British Academy, London, 1934.

Talmud Bavli (= Babylonian Talmud) in 18 volumes, Rosenkrantz & Schriftz-
ezer Press, Vilna, 1903.

Thomas, Cyrus, *Twelfth Annual Report of the Bureau of Ethnology to the
Secretary of the Smithsonian Institution 1890–'91*, Government Printing
Office, Washington, D.C., 1894.

Thompson, J. Eric S., *Maya Hieroglyphic Writing: Introduction*, Carnegie Institution of Washington, Washington, D.C., 1950.

Topp, Celia, *Pre-Historic Malta and Gozo*, Progress Press, Valetta (Malta),
no date.

Trump, D. H., *National Museum of Malta: Archaeological Section*, no date.

Wright, G. Ernest, *Biblical Archaeology*, Westminster Press, Philadelphia, 1957.

Wuthenau, Alexander von, *The Art of Terracotta Pottery in Pre-Columbian
Central and South America*, Crown Publishers, Inc., New York, 1970.

Zammit, T., *The Copper Age Temples of Hal-Tarxien*, 4th ed., Malta, 1966.

INDEX